Open Mind

Elementary Student's Book

Mickey Rogers
Joanne Taylore-Knowles
Steve Taylore-Knowles

Concept development:
Mariela Gil Vierma

MACMILLAN

Contents

GRAMMAR REVIEW: page 6

UNIT OPENER FUNCTIONS: giving personal details (1), making and checking guesses (2), talking about routines (3), asking for and giving opinions (4), expressing opinions (5), talking about lifestyles (6)

PRONUNCIATION	GRAMMAR	VOCABULARY	LIFESKILLS
SOUNDS: the alphabet	BE – STATEMENTS AND YES/NO QUESTIONS FUNCTION using be to give personal information such as name, age and nationality BE – WH- QUESTIONS: FUNCTION using be to ask for personal information such as name, age and nationality	USEFUL QUESTIONS FUNCTION using questions to ask for help in class ORDINAL NUMBERS FUNCTION using ordinal numbers to talk about dates	SELF AND SOCIETY: understanding forms FUNCTION identifying the correct personal information to complete a form
		LANGUAGE WRAP-UP	
WORDS: two-syllable nouns	ARTICLES FUNCTION using articles to describe people and organisations POSSESSION FUNCTION using the apostrophe, possessive adjectives, whose and have got to talk about family and relationships	OCCUPATIONS FUNCTION learning to talk about occupations FAMILY MEMBERS FUNCTION learning to talk about families	WORK AND CAREER: categorising FUNCTION categorising different jobs to work out the most suitable career
		LANGUAGE WRAP-UP	
SOUNDS: third person -s	PRESENT SIMPLE STATEMENTS AND YES/NO QUESTIONS FUNCTION using the present simple to talk about free-time activities PRESENT SIMPLE – INFORMATION QUESTIONS FUNCTION using the present simple to ask questions about people's habits and hobbies	FREE-TIME ACTIVITIES FUNCTION learning to talk about hobbies and free-time activities PERSONALITY ADJECTIVES FUNCTION using adjectives to describe people and what they like doing	STUDY AND LEARNING: understanding your learning style FUNCTION thinking about what you like doing to work out your learning style and improve how you learn English
		LANGUAGE WRAP-UP	
WORDS: days of the week	ADVERBS OF FREQUENCY FUNCTION using adverbs of frequency and adverbial phrases to talk about how often we do things CLAUSES WITH UNTIL, BEFORE AND AFTER FUNCTION using until, before and after to talk about sequences of events	TIME FUNCTION learning how to say what time it is PREPOSITIONS OF TIME FUNCTION using prepositions of time to talk about times of day, days of the week and sequences of activities	SELF AND SOCIETY: managing your time FUNCTION thinking about how you manage your time in order to prioritise different tasks
		LANGUAGE WRAP-UP	
WORDS: compound nouns	THERE IS / THERE ARE WITH SOME, ANY, SEVERAL, A LOT OF FUNCTION using there is / there are and quantifiers to describe places and attractions IMPERATIVE FUNCTION using the imperative to give instructions and directions to places in a city	PLACES AND ATTRACTIONS IN A CITY FUNCTION learning how to describe where you live LOCATIONS AND DIRECTIONS FUNCTION learning phrases to give directions to places	SELF AND SOCIETY: establishing priorities FUNCTION learning ways to study and practise listening
		LANGUAGE WRAP-UP	
SOUNDS: /ŋ/	PRESENT CONTINUOUS FUNCTION using the present continuous to talk about our lives PRESENT CONTINUOUS VS PRESENT SIMPLE FUNCTION using the present continuous and the present simple to talk about our lifestyles	LIFESTYLE ADJECTIVES FUNCTION using adjectives to describe different lifestyles A GREEN LIFESTYLE FUNCTION using verb collocations to describe a 'green' lifestyle	SELF AND SOCIETY: making personal change FUNCTION thinking about changes you want to make in your lifestyle
		LANGUAGE WRAP-UP	

	READING	LISTENING	SPEAKING	WRITING
UNIT 7 YOU'VE GOT TALENT page 80	**READING FOR THE MAIN IDEA:** a horoscope	Listening to a review of a TV show FUNCTIONS • describing talents and abilities • talking about likes and dislikes	**COMMUNICATION STRATEGY:** showing interest	Writing a personal reference **WRITING WORKSHOP** FUNCTIONS describing abilities and personal qualities
UNIT 8 SHOPPING AROUND page 92	Reading a questionnaire FUNCTIONS • talking about shopping habits • talking about how much things cost	**LISTENING FOR NUMERICAL INFORMATION:** product advertisements	Asking to try on clothes **SPEAKING WORKSHOP** FUNCTIONS • asking for help in a shop • talking about how much things cost	**WRITING COMPOUND SENTENCES:** using conjunctions to connect phrases (*and, or, but*)
UNIT 9 LET'S EAT page 104	**SCANNING FOR SPECIFIC INFORMATION:** restaurant advertisements	Listening to and taking phone messages FUNCTIONS • understanding phone language • making plans to go out	**COMMUNICATION STRATEGY:** using phone language	Writing a restaurant review **WRITING WORKSHOP** FUNCTIONS • describing different kinds of restaurants • giving opinions and making a recommendation
UNIT 10 SPEAKING OF THE PAST page 116	Reading a survey FUNCTION describing past experiences	**UNDERSTANDING THE MAIN IDEA:** informal conversations	Talking about a past experience **SPEAKING WORKSHOP** FUNCTION describing feelings towards past experiences	**SEQUENCING AND CONNECTING IDEAS:** using connectives like *first, then, after that* and *finally* to sequence ideas in a text
UNIT 11 GREAT LIVES page 128	**SCANNING FOR SPECIFIC INFORMATION:** a short biography	Listening to a life story FUNCTIONS • understanding biographical information • identifying key events in a person's life	**COMMUNICATION STRATEGY:** taking time to think	Writing a short biography **WRITING WORKSHOP** FUNCTIONS • recounting biographical information • talking about historical figures and events
UNIT 12 IN THE NEAR FUTURE page 140	Reading a blog FUNCTION thinking about intentions and resolutions	**UNDERSTANDING THE MAIN IDEA:** an informal conversation	Talking about plans and intentions **SPEAKING WORKSHOP** FUNCTION describing holiday plans	**SEQUENCING AND CONNECTING IDEAS:** using connectives like *first, then, next, after that* and *finally* to sequence ideas in a text

UNIT OPENER FUNCTIONS: talking about yourself (7), talking about likes and dislikes (8), expressing opinions (9), discussing results (10), comparing (11), talking about yourself (12)

PRONUNCIATION	GRAMMAR	VOCABULARY	LIFESKILLS
WORDS: can/can't	CAN/CAN'T FUNCTION using can and can't to talk about abilities ADVERBS OF MANNER FUNCTION using adverbs of manner to talk about people's talents	PERSONALITY ADJECTIVES FUNCTION using adjectives to describe people TALENTS AND ABILITIES FUNCTION learning to talk about what people are able to do	WORK AND CAREER: working as a team to complete a task FUNCTION identifying strengths and weaknesses of each member of the team, to ensure that tasks are completed efficiently
	LANGUAGE WRAP-UP		
SENTENCE RHYTHM: emphasis with this, that, these and those	DEMONSTRATIVE ADJECTIVES FUNCTION using this, that, these and those to identify items of clothing COMPARATIVE ADJECTIVES FUNCTION using comparative adjectives to compare gadgets	CLOTHES FUNCTION learning to talk about what people wear TECHNOLOGY ADJECTIVES FUNCTION using adjectives to talk about gadgets	WORK AND CAREER: making choices FUNCTION comparing different options to be able to make good choices
	LANGUAGE WRAP-UP		
SENTENCE RHYTHM: weak to	COUNTABLE AND UNCOUNTABLE NOUNS WITH SOME, ANY, MUCH AND MANY FUNCTION using quantifiers to talk about different amounts of food and drink items VERB PHRASES FUNCTION using phrases like I'd like to, let's and I have to to make, accept and refuse invitations and suggestions and to express obligations	FOOD FUNCTION learning to talk about different food and drink items and food groups ORDERING FOOD FUNCTION learning how to interpret menus and phrases to order food from a waiter	SELF AND SOCIETY: making a plan FUNCTION making a plan to be able to host a group meal
	LANGUAGE WRAP-UP		
SOUNDS: -ed endings	PAST SIMPLE – AFFIRMATIVE STATEMENTS FUNCTION using the past simple to describe a holiday PAST SIMPLE – QUESTIONS AND NEGATIVE STATEMENTS FUNCTION using the past simple to ask about somebody's weekend	-ED AND -ING ADJECTIVES FUNCTION using adjectives to talk about feelings and states MEMORABLE EXPERIENCES FUNCTION using verb collocations to talk about past experiences	STUDY AND LEARNING: making notes on a text FUNCTION identifying the most important information in a description of historical events
	LANGUAGE WRAP-UP		
SENTENCE RHYTHM: object pronouns	PAST SIMPLE WITH WHEN CLAUSES FUNCTION using the past simple with when to talk about the order of events in the past DIRECT AND INDIRECT OBJECTS FUNCTION using object pronouns to avoid repeating nouns in a description of a person's life	LIFE EVENTS FUNCTION learning to talk about key events in people's lives HISTORICAL EVENTS FUNCTION learning to talk about key events in history	STUDY AND LEARNING: brainstorming in a group FUNCTION brainstorming to come up with ideas for subjects for a biography
	LANGUAGE WRAP-UP		
WORDS: verbs ending in -y +ing	PRESENT CONTINUOUS AS FUTURE FUNCTION using the present continuous to talk about future plans and arrangements GOING TO FUTURE FUNCTION using going to to talk about future plans, intentions and resolutions	PHRASES WITH GO FUNCTION using present participles and the verb go to talk about activities INTENTIONS FUNCTION using start and stop + gerund to talk about good and bad habits and intentions for the future	STUDY AND LEARNING: identifying strengths and weaknesses FUNCTION evaluating areas for future improvement in learning English
	LANGUAGE WRAP-UP		

GRAMMAR REFERENCE: page 152   **IRREGULAR VERBS AND PRONUNCIATION SYMBOLS:** page 168

AUDIOSCRIPT: page 169   **ANSWER KEYS:** page 172

Grammar Review

1 **Choose the correct option to complete the sentences.**

1 My name are / is Jake.
2 How old are / is he?
3 Jenna and I are / is not late for class.
4 What is / are your phone number?
5 Mr Richards and Miss Green is / are teachers at my school.
6 Where is / are your brothers?

2 **Complete the sentences with the correct possessive adjective.**

1 They are Rachael and Daniel. _____ brother's name is Tony.
2 I play three sports. _____ favourite sport is tennis.
3 I'm from Colombia. _____ capital city is Bogotá.
4 This is Suzanna. _____ surname is Martin.
5 This is Jason. _____ mobile number is 07778965623.
6 'What's _____ email address?' 'My email address is ellieroisin@master.com'.

3 **Look at the picture. Complete the sentences with is or *are*.**

1 There _____ a mobile phone.
2 There _____ three _____.
3 There _____ a camera.
4 There _____ books.
5 There _____ a key.
6 There _____ a watch.

4 **Complete the sentences with *a, an, the* or – (no article).**

A: What's in the box?
B: I can see (1) _____ DVD, (2) _____ umbrella, and (3) _____ backpacks.
A: What colour is (4) _____ umbrella?
B: It's blue. (5) _____ backpacks are really cool. They're red and blue.
A: What's (6) _____ DVD about?
B: It's about (7) _____ artist from Spain.

5 **Complete the questions with the question words from the box.**

| What (x 2)   Who   How   Where   When |

1 _____ is your teacher?
2 _____ do you spell your name?
3 _____ are you from?
4 _____ is your email address?
5 _____ languages do they speak?
6 _____ do you do your homework?

6 **Put the words in the correct order to form questions.**

1 you / how / your / do / surname / pronounce / ?
2 from / where / your / sister's / husband / is / ?
3 speak / you / can / Italian / ?
4 time / does / lesson / what / finish / your / ?
5 lunch / you / have / what / do / for / ?
6 like / does / Kelly / job / her / ?

7 Look at the table. Complete the sentences with *can/can't* and a verb from the table.

	cook a paella	ride a bike	speak Spanish
Me	✗	✓	✗
Christian	✓	✓	✗
Marion	✓	✗	✓

1 Christian and I _____ Spanish.
2 Christian and Marion _____ a paella.
3 Christian and I _____ a bike.
4 Marion _____ a bike.
5 I _____ a paella.
6 Marion _____ Spanish.

8 Complete the questions 1–6. Then match them to the answers a–f.

1 _Does_ Margarita play the guitar?
2 _Are_ you a student?
3 _Is_ Jim busy?
4 _____ Henry drive a black car?
5 _____ David and Sara read Arabic?
6 _____ you have an email account?

a) No, I'm not.
b) No, he doesn't.
c) Yes, they do.
d) Yes, she does.
e) No, I don't.
f) Yes, he is.

9 Complete the sentences with the correct form of the verb in brackets.

1 Silvia and her mum _____ (*not be*) teachers.
2 Jack's wife _____ (*not like*) her job in the restaurant.
3 We _____ (*work*) from ten until nine.
4 I _____ (*not have*) a middle name.
5 The film _____ (*finish*) at 8 o'clock.
6 Marc's dad _____ (*go*) to work every day.

10 Circle the mistake and write the correct sentence on the line.

1 He's parents are engineers. _____
2 Katya favourite hobby is skiing. _____
3 Ours names are Jessica and Ben. _____
4 My parents friend's are from Japan. _____
5 They can watch a film at Michaels house. _____
6 Hers brother's home is in Sydney, Australia. _____

11 Rewrite the sentences using contractions where possible.

1 Hi! My nickname is Dev. _____
2 They are not expensive. _____
3 What time is your train? _____
4 Martin is not busy. _____
5 What are your favourite CDs? _____
6 When is your class? _____
7 The umbrellas are under the desk. _____
8 There is a sale at the supermarket. _____

12 Look at the frequency adverb thermometer on the right and put the words from the box in the correct place in the sentences. Change the verb form if necessary.

usually   never   sometimes   always   often   rarely

1 Caroline's sister / check / her email / every day.
2 I / drink / coffee / in / the / afternoon.
3 Joe / watch / TV / on / Sunday / morning.
4 Lindsey and Julia / get up / late / during the / week.
5 She / write / a diary / at the weekend.
6 I / spend / a lot / of / time / on / the phone.

UNIT 1 NICE TO MEET YOU!

READING
recognising cognates
What words in English do you know that are the same (or almost the same) as words in your language?

SPEAKING
using polite language
What polite words or phrases in English, such as *please*, do you know?

LIFE SKILLS
SELF & SOCIETY

understanding forms In which situations do people complete forms? Think of as many situations as you can. What different kinds of forms can you find in this unit?

A Look at the photos. Who is asking for personal information? Who is giving personal information? Label the boxes A, B or A/B if both are possible.

1 a job interview
☐ give personal information
☐ ask about personal information

2 a party
☐ give personal information
☐ ask about personal information

3 a language institute
☐ give personal information
☐ ask about personal information

HOW TO SAY IT

Giving personal details
My name is ...
I'm from ...
I'm ... years old.
I'm interested in ...

B Work in pairs. Roleplay a conversation at a party. You meet someone you don't know. Tell him/her about yourself and ask questions to find out about him/her.

A: *Hello! My name's Aidan.*
B: *Oh, hello, Aidan. Nice to meet you. I'm Jenny.*

A Look at this webpage. Who is it for?

MyFriends.com
AN INTERNATIONAL SOCIAL SITE FOR STUDENTS OF ENGLISH

HOME   ACCOUNT   LOGIN   ENTER SURVEY

Contact people in other countries.
Communicate in English.
Complete the registration form below and join us!

First name	Username
Surname	Password
Country	Security question
Email address	When is your birthday?
Telephone number	e.g. 19th March 1991

Next

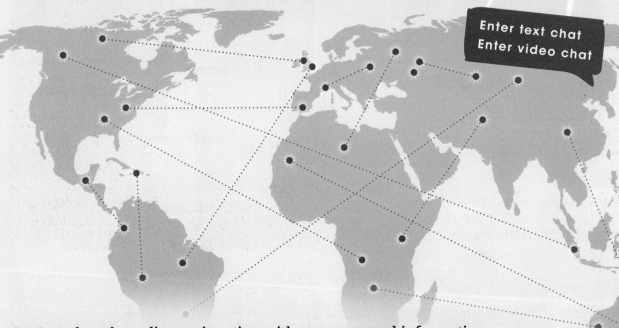

Enter text chat
Enter video chat

B Complete the online registration with your personal information.
What's your username? What's your password?

Many words are similar in different languages. Look for these words when you read.
Use them to help you understand the text.

A Read the survey on the next page. (Circle) the words you recognise.
How many words are similar in your language?

B Complete the survey.

MyFriends Personal Profile Survey

Find friends similar to you. We have students from all over the world.
Complete the survey with information about yourself and click send.

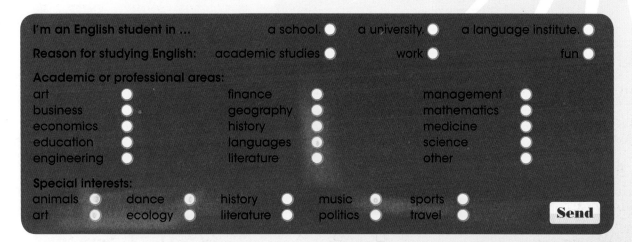

I'm an English student in ...   a school. ○   a university. ○   a language institute. ○

Reason for studying English: academic studies ○   work ○   fun ○

Academic or professional areas:

art ○	finance ○	management ○
business ○	geography ○	mathematics ○
economics ○	history ○	medicine ○
education ○	languages ○	science ○
engineering ○	literature ○	other ○

Special interests:

animals ○	dance ○	history ○	music ○	sports ○
art ○	ecology ○	literature ○	politics ○	travel ○

Send

VOCABULARY: useful questions

A »🎧01 **Listen and repeat the questions.**

- Can you help me?
- Can you speak more slowly?
- How do you say that in English?
- Can you spell that?
- Can you repeat that?
- What does that mean?

B Some of these phrases are also useful outside the classroom. For photos 1–4, say which questions are possible. Check with a partner.

GRAMMAR: *be* – statements and *Yes/No* questions

A LANGUAGE IN CONTEXT Read this conversation. Complete the statements.

Professor Brown: Hi, everyone. Welcome. I am Professor Brown. Please say a few words about yourself.

Brooke: Hi. I'm Brooke. I'm from New York and I'm 20 years old.

Anka: Hello, everyone. I'm Anka, I'm 21 and I'm from Poland.

Professor Brown: Are you from Warsaw, Anka?

Anka: No, I'm not. I'm from Gdansk.

Professor Brown: Is Gdansk a big city?

Anka: Yes, it is! It's very big.

Professor Brown: Thanks. Next?

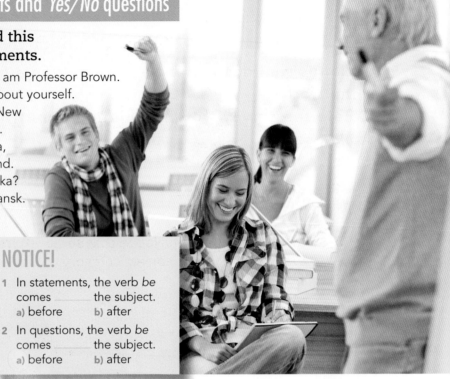

1 Brooke is from _____.
2 Anka is _____ years old.

NOTICE!

1 In statements, the verb *be* comes _____ the subject.
   a) before   b) after

2 In questions, the verb *be* comes _____ the subject.
   a) before   b) after

B ANALYSE Read the conversation in Exercise A again.

Form Complete the tables with words from the conversation.

Statements with *be*

Affirmative				Negative			
I	(1) _____	(I'm)		I	am not	(I'm not)	
You/We/They	are	(You're/We're/They're)	from Gdansk.	You/We/They	are not	(You/We/They aren't)	from Warsaw.
He/She/It	(2) _____	(He's/She's/It's)		He/She/It	is not	(He/She/It isn't)	

Yes/No questions with *be*		Short answers
(3) _____ you/they	from Poland?	Yes, I am. / No, I'm not.
		Yes, we/they are. / No, we/they aren't.
Is he/she/it		Yes, he/she/it is. / No, he/she/it isn't.

Function Choose the correct option to complete the sentence.

We use the verb *be* to talk about ...
a) people and things and facts about them, such as age, name, etc.
b) things we do every day.

C PRACTISE Choose the correct options to complete the sentences.

1 Jack and Sarah are / am in Europe.
2 Is / Are you a music student?
3 John isn't / aren't here.
4 We are / is university students.
5 Is / Am she 19 years old?
6 Ed and Isabelle isn't / aren't from the USA.
7 I are / am 22.
8 Is / Are Eva from Spain?

WHAT'S RIGHT?
◯ Yes, we're.
◯ Yes, we are.

WHAT'S RIGHT?
◯ I am 20 years old.
◯ I have 20 years.

D **NOW YOU DO IT** Work in pairs. Choose two of the people below. Roleplay a conversation like the one in Exercise A.

Stefano, 19
Rome, Italy

Ana, 24
Madrid, Spain

Devesh, 23
New Delhi, India

Isabela, 21
São Paulo, Brazil

PRONUNCIATION: the alphabet

A 🎧 02 Listen to the alphabet. Notice that some letters have similar sounds. Write each letter in the correct category.

A̶ B̶ C D E E̶ G H I̶ J K L M N O̶ P Q̶ R̶ S T U V W X Y Z

/eɪ/	/iː/	/e/	/aɪ/	/əʊ/	/juː/	/ɑː/
A	B	F	I	O	Q	R

B Work in pairs. Choose a word from this unit, or another English word you know. Spell it for your partner to guess the word.

SPEAKING: using polite language

⚙ Use *excuse me*, *thank you*, *thanks*, *you're welcome*, and *please* to be polite in English.

A 🎧 03 Listen to the conversation below. <u>Underline</u> the polite language.

Luke: Excuse me, can I get your information, please? What's your name?
Simon: It's Simon Whitfield.
Luke: Can you spell your surname, please?
Simon: It's W-H-I-T-F-I-E-L-D.
Luke: Thanks. Now, what's your email address?
Simon: It's simonw@mail.com.
Luke: And your phone number?
Simon: It's 04 141 278 454.
Luke: Thank you very much.
Simon: You're welcome.

B Make a mini class directory in your notebook. Work in groups. Ask your classmates for their information. Include their first name, surname, email address and phone number. Use polite language.

HOW TO SAY IT

In email addresses:
@ say *at*
. say *dot*

Nice to meet you! | **UNIT 1** | 13

VOCABULARY: ordinal numbers

A Write the correct ordinal number next to each word.

first	1st	nineteenth	_____	fifth	_____
seventh	_____	third	_____	thirteenth	_____
eleventh	_____	tenth	10th	ninth	_____
fourteenth	_____	thirtieth	_____	twentieth	_____
sixth	_____	twenty-fifth	_____	eighth	_____
fifteenth	_____	twelfth	_____		
fourth	_____	second	2nd		

HOW TO SAY IT

Ordinal numbers:

We say: first, second, tenth, twentieth

We write: 1st, 2nd, 10th, 20th

Dates:

We say: The second of October, 2016. Tuesday is the second of October/October the second.

We write: 02/10/16, Tuesday is 2nd October.

B Complete these sentences with names of days, months and ordinal numbers as appropriate.

1 Halloween is _____ October.
2 Today is _____ .
3 Next Friday is _____ .
4 Valentine's Day is _____ February.
5 New Year's Day is _____ January.
6 My birthday is on _____ .

GRAMMAR: *be – wh-* questions

A 🎧 **04 LANGUAGE IN CONTEXT** Listen to the conversation. Complete the sentences.

Assistant: I need to take your personal details. First of all, what's your name?
Jordan: Jordan Turner.
Assistant: And where are you from?
Jordan: Norwich.
Assistant: How old are you, Jordan?
Jordan: I'm 20.
Assistant: And when is your birthday?
Jordan: 11th July.
Assistant: Thank you. Now, I need you to sign here ...

1 Jordan is _____ years old.
2 His birthday is in the month of _____ .

NOTICE!

1 <u>Underline</u> these words and phrases in the conversation:

what	where	how	old	when

2 They come _____ the verb *be*.
   a) before   b) after

14

B ANALYSE Read the conversation in Exercise A again.

Form Choose the correct option to complete the sentences.
Wh- question words and phrases come **(1)** at the beginning / at the end of a question.
Then, we put **(2)** the verb *be* / the subject of the sentence.

Function Complete the table with words from the conversation.

Question word	Use	Example
(1) *what*	things	**(5)** _____ *your name?*
(2) _____	places	**(6)** _____ *you from?*
(3) _____	dates	**(7)** _____ *your birthday?*
(4) _____	someone's age	**(8)** _____ *you?*

C PRACTISE Read these answers. Write questions for the answers.

1 **A:** *What's your surname?*   **B:** My surname is Henning.
2 **A:** _____ ?   **B:** I'm 21. And you?
3 **A:** _____ ?   **B:** 8th September.
4 **A:** _____ ?   **B:** I'm from Austria. What about you?
5 **A:** _____ ?   **B:** My brother? He's 30 years old.
6 **A:** _____ ?   **B:** His name is George.

D NOW YOU DO IT Ask your classmates questions from Exercise C
and complete this table.

Find someone ...	Name
with a birthday in the same month as yours.	
from another town or country.	
with a surname beginning with the same letter as yours.	

LISTENING: to a voicemail message

A 05 Listen to this voicemail message. Choose the
correct option to complete the sentences.

1 The message is from ...
   a) Laura.   b) Paula.   c) Carla.
2 Her birthday is on ... August.
   a) 8th   b) 18th   c) 28th
3 Her party is at the ... Club.
   a) Clinton   b) Klinton   c) Clintern
4 Her party is at ... o'clock.
   a) five   b) nine   c) seven

B Work in pairs. Follow the instructions below.

• Student A, it's your birthday! Think about the date, location
  and time of your party. Call your friend and leave a message.
• Student B, listen to the message and write the details.
• When you finish, switch roles.

The party is on
It's at
Be there at

Nice to meet you!

LifeSkills

UNDERSTANDING FORMS

- Identify the type of form.
- Complete the parts you understand.
- Ask for help with parts you don't understand.

A **Where do you complete forms in English? Match the phrases to the correct picture.**

a) at a hotel ☐
b) at the airport ☐
c) on a website ☐
d) at a language institute ☐

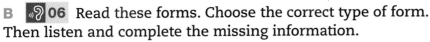

B **06 Read these forms. Choose the correct type of form. Then listen and complete the missing information.**

The Royal Wellington		Tel: +44 (0) 21 7441 6333	
67 Wellington Square		Fax: +44 (0) 21 5654 2323	
London NW2 6AR		Email: royalwellington@mailnet.co.uk	

Full Name	Yousef Mahuad	Smoking room	☐
Date of Birth	05/12/1990	Non-smoking room	✓
Date of Arrival	17ᵗʰ June	Single room	✓
Date of Departure		Double room	☐

1 This is a hotel registration form / a library application form.

Make a payment

Full name	Card type
Yousef Mahuad	VISA
Email address	**Card number**
yousefm1990@mymail.com	4972334333217174
	Expiry date / **Security code**
	31/12/2018

2 This is a library registration form / a credit card payment form.

C Look at this United Kingdom immigration form. Complete the information in items 1.4, 1.5, 1.6 and 1.11.

D Work in pairs. Roleplay asking each other questions about the other information on the form.

Home Office
UK Border Agency

Section 1: Personal Information

1.1 Please give previous Immigration and Nationality Directorate or Border and Immigration Agency or UK Border Agency reference numbers

1.2 Current passport/travel document number

1.3 Please say when you were given indefinite leave to enter/remain in the UK (not necessary if you are a Commonwealth citizen with right of abode in the United Kingdom). If you are an EEA national, a Swiss national or a family member of an EEA or Swiss national you should read pages 8-10 of the Booklet AN.

D D   M M   Y Y Y Y

1.4 ✔ Title   Mr ☐   Mrs ☐   Miss ☐   Ms ☐   Other Title ➤

1.5 Surname/Family Name (Please note: The name you give here will be the name shown on your certificate so please ensure it is spelt correctly and you have written it in the correct order.)

1.6 Other names (Please note: Your name will be shown on your certificate so please ensure it is spelt correctly and you have written it in the correct order. We would expect this to be the same as on your official documents. If this name is not the name used on your current passport or travel document, or is spelt differently, you must explain why on page 13)

1.7 Name at birth if different from above. (If the names you have given are different or spelt differently from the name shown on your passport, please explain why on page 13)

1.8 If you are or have ever been known by any name or names apart from those mentioned above, please give details here.

1.9 Your present nationality

1.10 National Insurance Number

1.11 Date of birth
D D   M M   Y Y Y Y

1.12 Village or town or city of birth

1.13 Country of birth

1.14 Sex (Please tick (✔) appropiate box)   Male ☐   Female ☐

1.15 Current marital / civil partnership status (Please tick (✔) one box only)

Are you: Married? ☐   In a civil partnership? ☐

Divorced? ☐   Widowed? ☐   Civil partnership dissolved? ☐

Legally separated? ☐   Single/Never married? ☑

1.16 Present address *You must give us any change of address in writing while we are considering this application.*

Postcode

Please state the date that you moved into this address
D D   M M   Y Y Y Y

Contact Details

Daytime/mobile telephone number

Evening telephone number

e-mail address

? **REFLECT …** How can the skill of understanding forms be useful to you in **Work and Career** and **Study and Learning**?

Language wrap-up

1 VOCABULARY

A Complete the conversations with words from the box. **(5 points)**

slowly   repeat   say   help   spell

1	A: Can you _____ me? This is very difficult.	B: Yes, of course.
2	A: How do you _____ that in English?	B: You say, 'Excuse me.'
3	A: Can you speak more _____, please?	B: Yes, I'm sorry.
4	A: How do you _____ your name?	B: It's P - E - N - E - L - O - P - E.
5	A: Sorry, can you _____ that, please?	B: Yes. P - E - N - E - L - O - P - E.

B Complete the sentences with the ordinal numbers for the words in brackets. **(5 points)**

1 Today is _____ August. (*twenty-third*)
2 Tomorrow is the _____. (*fourteenth*)
3 _____ April is April Fool's Day in the UK. (*first*)
4 On _____ November, people in the UK celebrate Bonfire Night. (*fifth*)
5 Wednesday is _____ May. (*second*)

8 – 10 correct: I can ask useful questions and use ordinal numbers.
0 – 7 correct: Look again at the Vocabulary sections on pages 11 and 14.
SCORE: /10

2 GRAMMAR

Alexandra is from the UK. She is introducing herself to a new friend in Argentina.
Read her email. Choose the correct options to complete the text. **(10 points)**

To:	carolina_borges@mymail.com
From:	alex_brown@mymail.com
Subject:	Hi

Hi Carolina,

My name **(1)** am / is / are Alexandra and I **(2)** am / is / are from Leicester, in the UK. I'm 19 – my birthday **(3)** am / is / are in May. I **(4)** am / is / are a university student – I study biology. My friends at university **(5)** am / is / are Jessica, Sophie, and Hannah. Jessica and Sophie **(6)** am / is / are 19 and Hannah is 18. What about you? **(7)** What / Where / How old are you? **(8)** What / Where / When is your birthday? **(9)** What / Where / When exactly are you from in Argentina – is it Buenos Aires? **(10)** What / Where / When are the names of your friends?

I hope you answer my email!

Your new friend,

Alexandra

8 – 10 correct: I can use *be* in statements and ask questions to get information about people.
0 – 7 correct: Look again at the Grammar sections on pages 12 and 14.
SCORE: /10

WRITING WORKSHOP

A Look at this online registration form and answer these questions.

1 What course is this person on? _____
2 Where is this person from? _____
3 What are this person's interests? _____

Mansfield Institute New Student Registration

This page is for new students to register at Mansfield Institute.
For other enquiries, see the links below. ———————————— A

Home   About us   Courses   Fees   Contact us ———————————— B

Complete all boxes and submit. ———————————— C

Name:	Alice Kohl
Date of birth:	05/11/95
Country of origin:	Germany
Nationality:	German
Course:	BA Psychology
Interests:	reading, cinema, cooking, playing video games
Username:	akohl95
Password:	******

D

[Submit]   [Cancel] ———————————— E

B Look at the online registration form again. Decide which part of the registration form (A–E) does each of the following things.

This part of the form ...

1 gives you instructions. _____
2 says who this page is for. _____
3 has buttons to send your registration. _____
4 sends you to other pages. _____
5 asks for your details. _____

C NOW YOU DO IT Complete the registration form for yourself.

Complete all boxes and press submit.

Name:	
Date of birth:	
Country of origin:	
Nationality:	
Course:	
Interests:	
Username:	
Password:	

[Submit]   [Cancel]

HOW ARE YOU DOING?

Look back at your writing and tick the statements that are true.

○ My spelling is correct.
○ The form says what course I am on.
○ The form says what my interests are.
○ The right information is in the right boxes.

Now ask a partner to look at your writing and tick.

Is the personal information clear and correct?

● Well done!   ● Nearly! Look at the unit again.   ● Think again! Ask your teacher for help.

UNIT 2 WHAT DO YOU DO?

IN THIS UNIT YOU

- ⚙ learn language to talk about your family and occupations
- ⚙ listen to a conversation about occupations
- ⚙ learn to write sentences correctly
- ⚙ read about a famous person's occupation
- ⚙ have a conversation about your relatives and their occupations
- ⚙ learn to use categories to make a decision about your career
- ▶ watch a video about occupations

LISTENING
for specific information

When people talk about themselves, what kind of personal information do they often give? e.g. their name, ...

WRITING
understanding the mechanics

Are capital letters used in the same way in English and your language? With a partner, make a list of uses that are the same/different.

LIFE SKILLS

WORK & CAREER

categorising Play 'Categories'. One person names a category of things (e.g. *objects beginning with 'c'*). Everyone then names something in that category (e.g. *chair*). If you can't, you're out. The last person in is the winner.

A Match these famous people to their main profession.

1 ☐

A film director

2 ☐

B singer

3 ☐

C actor

B Each person also does another activity. Who is …

- a clothing designer?
- a musician?
- a pilot?

A: *I think Woody Allen is a pilot.*

B: *A pilot? Really?*

A Match the occupations to the photos.

1 G taxi driver *пробелиз*
2 E teacher
3 I actor
4 H firefighter
5 B police officer
6 A soldier
7 F doctor
8 C engineer
9 J lawyer
10 D writer

B Which of these occupations are dangerous? Number the red boxes from 1 (very dangerous) to 10 (not dangerous).

C 🔊 Work in pairs. Compare your choices. Do you agree or disagree?

A: *My number one is …*
B: *I agree.*

D 🔊 Now number the blue boxes from 1 (very interesting) to 10 (not interesting). Then work in pairs and compare your choices.

A 🎧 **07** Listen to the words. (Circle) the syllable that is stressed in each word.

doc–tor   tea–cher   law–yer

B 🔊 🎧 **08** Work in pairs. Practise saying these words. Make sure you stress the correct syllable. Listen and check.

singer   driver   writer   actor   soldier   dancer

GRAMMAR: articles

A LANGUAGE IN CONTEXT Read this text. What job or jobs does each person do?

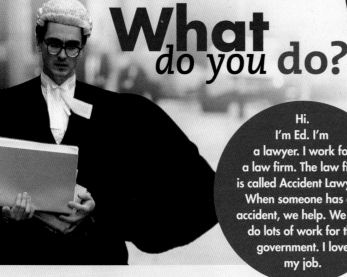

What
do you do?

I'm John and this is Carol. We're musicians. I'm a pianist and she's a singer. We're in a band called White Nights. The band is fun but hard work! Our next concert is at the Olympic® Park in Sydney!

Hi. I'm Ed. I'm a lawyer. I work for a law firm. The law firm is called Accident Lawyers. When someone has an accident, we help. We also do lots of work for the government. I love my job.

B ANALYSE Read the text in Exercise A again.

NOTICE!

(Circle) the words *a*, *an* and **the** in the text. What words come after them?

a) verbs   b) adjectives   (c)) nouns

Form

zero article	(no article)
indefinite article	*a/an*
definite article	*the*

WHAT'S RIGHT?

◐ My mother is a teacher.
○ My mother is teacher.

Function **Choose the correct options to complete the sentences.**

1 We use *a* before …
   a) singular nouns.   b) plural nouns.
2 We use *an* before singular nouns that begin with …
   a) a vowel.   b)) a consonant.
3 We use … before plural nouns for general reference.
   a) *the*   b) no (zero) article

4 We use *a* the first time we mention something, and then we use …
   a)) *an.*   b) *the.*
5 We use … before a thing, place or organisation there is only one of.
   a) *a*   b) *the*

C PRACTISE Complete the sentences with *a, an, the* or – (no article).

1 James is _a_ soldier.
2 Andy and Dave are _an_ teachers.
3 I want to be _an_ artist.
4 I'm in a band. _an_ band is called Love Hurts.

5 Lucy and I are _a_ musicians.
6 Are you _a_ singer?
7 Richard works in a hospital. What's _a_ hospital called?
8 Harry's a doctor in _an_ army.

D 🔊 **NOW YOU DO IT** Work in pairs. Ask and answer questions about the people in the pictures in Exercise A.

A: *What does he do?*   B: *He's a …*

What do you do? | **UNIT 2** | **23**

VOCABULARY: family members

A Look at this picture. Say what James, Sarah, Will, Cathy and Robert do.

James	Sarah	Will	Cathy	Robert	Rose	Brian
1 _police officer_	doctor	2 _fairman_	3 _mum_	5 _dad_ _driver_	6 _grandma_	7 _grandad_

4 _____ parents _____

B 🎧 **09** Listen to Sarah and write the correct word from the box under each name in Exercise A.

granddad   brother   boyfriend   dad   ~~parents~~   ~~mum~~   grandma

C 🎧 **10** Listen and match.

1 parents
2 brother
3 mum and dad
4 boyfriend
5 grandparents
6 wife

a) sister
b) girlfriend
c) grandchildren
d) children
e) husband
f) son and daughter

LISTENING: for specific information

Read the task before you listen. Think about what information you need. For example, is it a name or a place? Listen carefully for this information.

A Read these statements about Rachel. Choose the correct type of missing information.

1 Rachel is a _____.
The missing information is her occupation / her full name.
2 Her job is very _____.
The missing information is a noun / an adjective.
3 Her day usually starts at _____ o'clock.
The missing information is a name / a time.
4 Her _____ is a firefighter.
The missing information is a place / a family member.

B 🎧 **11** Listen and complete the sentences in Exercise A with one word.

C 🎧 **12** Listen to this conversation between Rachel and a friend. Complete the sentences.

1 Rachel's friend is a _____.
2 She works in an _____.
3 She thinks her job is very _____.
4 Her sister is a _____.

READING: a celebrity biography

A Many actors come from acting families. Is this true in your country?

B Read the biography. Answer the questions.

SPANISH STAR
IN HOLLYWOOD
by Emma Spires

Javier Bardem is an actor from Spain. He comes from an acting family. Some of his relatives are actors. His mother (Pilar Bardem) is an actor, and his uncle (Juan Antonio Bardem) was a film director. His brother Carlos and his sister Monica are both actors.

Javier is famous in both the Spanish-speaking world and the English-speaking world. He has many awards, including an Oscar® and a Golden Globe® award for his role in *No Country for Old Men*.

1 Where is Javier Bardem from? _Spain_
2 What do his brother and sister do? _actors_
3 What awards does Javier Bardem have? _Oscar and Golden Globe®_

C Work in groups. Do you know people who have similar occupations to other members of their family? Think of as many as you can and compare.

My sister, my dad, and my mum are engineers.

WRITING: understanding the mechanics

Use a capital letter at the beginning of every sentence, and a full stop (.), exclamation mark (!), or question mark (?) at the end of every sentence. Also use capital letters for the word *I*, for the names of people and places, for countries, nationalities and languages, and for months and days of the week.

A Circle nine mistakes in the sentences below.

1 My brother is in egypt.   *Egypt*
4 I start my new job on wednesday.   *W*
2 Today is 14ᵗʰ february.
5 How do you say this in english   *E*
3 My sister and i are dentists   *I*
6 how old is your brother, peter?   *How   Peter*

B Write sentences to answer these questions. Be careful with capital letters and punctuation.

1 What do you do? _I do my homework._
2 What day is it today? _It is a Friday_
3 What month is it? _It is a December_
4 Who is your favourite relative? _____

GRAMMAR: possession

A LANGUAGE IN CONTEXT Read the information below and choose T (true) or F (false).

Hi, I'm Liam. I haven't got any brothers, but I've got two sisters. Their names are Sam and Jodie, and they're very different! Sam has got brown hair and her eyes are brown. Jodie's eyes are brown, too. But Jodie hasn't got brown hair – hers is blonde. Sam's a teacher and she loves her job. Jodie's a manager. Whose job is the best? Mine is! I'm a singer. I'm in a band with some friends. Our band isn't famous, but who knows? Maybe one day …

1	Liam, Sam and Jodie are relatives.	T / F
2	Sam and Jodie do the same job.	T / F

B ANALYSE Read the text in Exercise A again.

Form Complete the tables with words from the text.

NOTICE!

(Circle) the ways of talking about possession that you recognise in the paragraph. What are they?

have got

Affirmative		Negative
I have got	(1) _____	I (3) _____
You have got	You've got	You haven't got
He/She/It (2) *had* got	He/She/It's got	He/She/It hasn't got
We have got	We've got	We haven't got
They have got	They've got	They haven't got

possessive apostrophe

Add 's	Add ' after s
Singular nouns	**Regular plural nouns**
e.g. Jodie's eyes	e.g. my parents' house
my sister's job (= the job of my sister)	my sisters' jobs (= the jobs of my sisters)
Irregular plural nouns	
e.g. the children's rooms	
women's rights	

Remember that 's is also the contraction for *is*
Jodie's a manager = Jodie is a manager NOT A manager of Jodie
Sam's a teacher = Sam is a teacher NOT A teacher of Sam

WHAT'S RIGHT?
- My sisters are both student's.
- My sisters are both students.

whose

whose + noun + verb
e.g. Whose job (4) _____ the best?

WHAT'S RIGHT?
- ✓ That pen is mine.
- That pen is my.

possessive pronouns

I	you	he	she	we	you	they
(5) _____	yours	his	(6) _____	ours	yours	theirs

e.g.
This is <u>my bag</u>. That is <u>your bag</u>.
This is <u>mine</u>. That is <u>yours</u>.

Function Match 1–4 with a–d to complete the sentences.

1 We use *have*   a) instead of a noun to talk about possession.
2 We use *'s* or *'* after a noun to   b) ask about possession.
3 We use possessive pronouns   c) *got* to talk about things people possess or own.
4 We use *whose* to   d) say who something belongs to.

C   **PRACTISE**   Choose the correct option to complete the sentences.

1 My parents' / parent's jobs are very interesting.
2 I haven't / hasn't got any brothers or sisters.
3 Who / Whose mobile phone is this?
4 Is that Rob's / Robs' laptop on the table?
5 Holly's / Holly got a really good job.
6 Your book is over there. This one is my / mine.
7 The Coen brother's / brothers' new film is great.
8 Ewan and Will think our house is like them / theirs.
9 Whose brother is / is brother called Oliver?
10 Those are all my family photos. Now show me you / yours.

D   **NOW YOU DO IT**   Say what you know about these people. Say what their relatives do. Work in pairs.

Owen and Luke Wilson

Sofia and Francis Ford Coppola

Will Smith and Jada Pinkett-Smith

Sofia's dad is a film director. She's got two children and a brother. Her brother is also a film director.

SPEAKING: talking about family

A   **13** Listen to the conversation below. Answer the questions.

Sam: So, tell me a bit about your family.
Lauren: Well, my brother Matt is a mechanic.
Sam: And your sister?
Lauren: Nicola's a teacher.
Sam: Are they married?
Lauren: Yes, my brother's wife is a taxi driver, and Nicola's husband is a police officer.
Sam: What about your parents?
Lauren: Mum's a shop assistant and Dad's a lawyer. What about your family?

1 What does Lauren's sister do?
2 What does her mum do?

B   Draw your family tree in your notebook.

C   Work in pairs. Ask and answer questions about your relatives and their occupations.

A: *What does your mum do?*
B: *She's a …*

WHAT'S RIGHT?
☑ Lauren's sister
○ the sister of Lauren

LifeSkills

CATEGORISING

- Understand the purpose of categorising.
- Categorise the items using relevant characteristics.
- Use the information to make a decision.

A Look at the website on the next page. Who is it for? Choose the correct option.

This website is for people who …

a) want to find their ideal job.

b) want to find someone to do a job.

B Work in pairs. Write these careers in the different categories below. Each career can be in more than one category.

architect

software engineer

sales manager

designer

journalist

mechanic

creative jobs: _____

well-paid jobs: _____

office jobs: _____

jobs working with others: _____

jobs requiring a physical skill: _____

jobs working from home: _____

C Complete this questionnaire for yourself.
You can choose more than one answer.

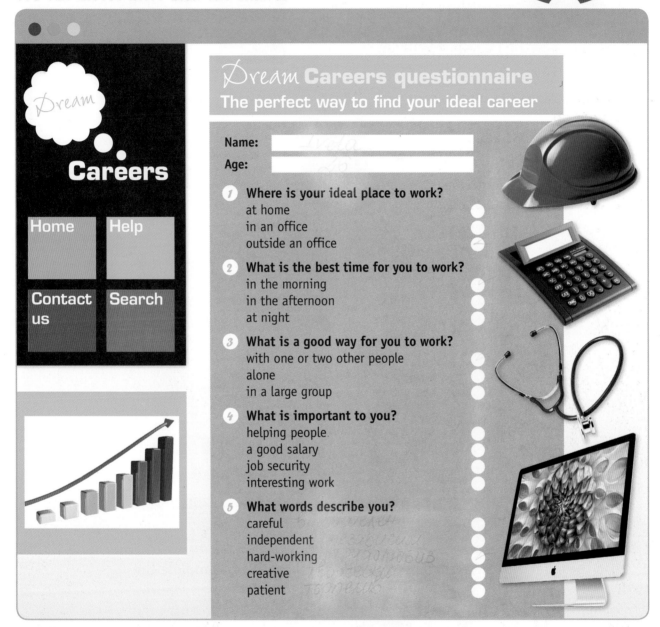

Dream Careers questionnaire
The perfect way to find your ideal career

Careers

Home   Help

Contact   Search
us

Name:
Age:

1. **Where is your ideal place to work?**
   at home
   in an office
   outside an office

2. **What is the best time for you to work?**
   in the morning
   in the afternoon
   at night

3. **What is a good way for you to work?**
   with one or two other people
   alone
   in a large group

4. **What is important to you?**
   helping people
   a good salary
   job security
   interesting work

5. **What words describe you?**
   careful
   independent
   hard-working
   creative
   patient

D Work in pairs. Compare your answers and complete the sentence below for your partner. Use the jobs in Exercise B and the rest of this unit to help you.

My partner's perfect for a career as a …

E Tell your classmates about your career recommendation for your partner.

Sally is perfect for a career as a …

REFLECT... How can the skill of categorising be useful to you in
Self and Society and **Study and Learning**?

Language wrap-up

1 VOCABULARY

Look at Mark's family tree. Then complete the sentences with one word. There are three jobs and seven family words. (10 points)

1 Edward and Liz are Mark's _____ .

2 Edward is Mark's _____ .

3 Liz is Mark's mum and Edward's _____ .

4 Mary and Suzie are Mark's _____ .

5 Ian is his _____ .

6 Mark is a _____ .

7 Suzie is a police _____ .

8 Sarah is Mary's _____ . She's eight years old.

9 George and Eleanor are Mark's _____ .

10 George is a taxi _____ .

 George
 Eleanor

 Edward
 Liz

 Mark
 Mary
 Suzie
 Ian

 Sarah

2 GRAMMAR

A Read these facts about famous people and their families. Complete the sentences with *a*, *an, the* or – (no article). (5 points)

Julio Iglesias is **(1)** _A_ famous singer. His sons, Enrique and Julio Iglesias Jr. are **(2)** _AN_ singers, too. Michael Douglas's wife, Catherine Zeta Jones, is **(3)** _AN_ actor. Michael's father, Kirk Douglas, is also **(4)** _AN_ actor. He was a sailor in **(5)** _THE_ navy, too!

B Choose the correct option to complete the sentences. (5 points)

1 Who / Whose daughter is Stella McCartney?

2 Martin Sheen's sons are actors, but most of them use a different surname from his / theirs.

3 George Clooney's / Clooneys' father is a famous TV host and writer.

4 Madonna's name is Italian, like my / mine.

5 Ben Affleck's children's / childrens' names are Violet, Seraphina, and Samuel.

A Read the conversation. Choose the correct option to complete the text.

Amber: Excuse me, but are you Jack's brother?

Lucas: Yes, I am. I'm Lucas. I'm a manager at Johnson's.

Amber: Hi! I'm Amber. I work with Jack at Webstart. He says he comes from quite a big family!

Lucas: That's right! There are seven of us, and Mum and Dad. What **(1)** with / about yours?

Amber: Oh, I've got a very small family. It's just me and **(2)** my / her mum and dad.

Lucas: Wow! I can't imagine that.

Amber: **(3)** Tell / Talk me about your brothers and sisters. What do they **(4)** do / make?

Lucas: Two of my sisters, Lola and Karen, are police **(5)** officers / fighters. My other sister, Ava, is **(6)** a / the teacher.

Amber: Really? My **(7)** dad / dad's a teacher. My mum works in a hospital. How about **(8)** your / yours mum?

Lucas: Mine doesn't work, so she's a stay-at-home mum, I suppose. My other sister's a stay-at-home mum, too. She **(9)** has / have got three kids.

Amber: That's four sisters, you and Jack …

Lucas: And my little brother, Andrew. He's still at university. So, what's it like being an only child?

Amber: Well, I suppose there are advantages and disadvantages …

B Find and <u>underline</u> the following things in the conversation.

1 a question about who someone is
2 two questions about family
3 two expressions of surprise
4 nine sentences that say what someone does
5 a question about life in someone's family

C Work in pairs. Imagine that you and your partner meet at an informal business event. Roleplay a conversation, asking each other about your families.

Things to include:
- greetings
- at least two questions about family
- at least two expressions of surprise
- sentences saying what different family members do
- at least one question about the other person's family life

D Now find a different person to talk to. Have a new conversation about your families with your partner. Try to remember to include things from the list in Exercise C.

HOW ARE YOU DOING?

Think about your speaking. Do you feel confident using:
○ greetings?
○ questions about the other person's family?
○ expressions of surprise?
○ statements about the occupations of family members?
How do you feel about your speaking generally?

⬤ ⬤ ⬤

Very confident. Not sure … Need to practise

UNIT 3 DOWN TIME

IN THIS UNIT YOU

- learn language to talk about habits and free-time activities
- read an article about celebrity hobbies
- practise asking for opinions on free-time activities
- listen to a radio show about a free-time activity
- write about yourself and your interests
- think about what you like doing in order to understand your learning style
- ▶ watch a video about different free-time activities

READING
recognising cognates
Can you find two words on each page of this unit that are similar to words in your language?

SPEAKING
asking for opinions
Before you see a new film, read a new book, or play a new video game, do you listen to other people's opinions first? Whose?

LIFE SKILLS

STUDY & LEARNING

understanding your learning style
How do you learn something new such as a new skill or a new word? Describe what you do.

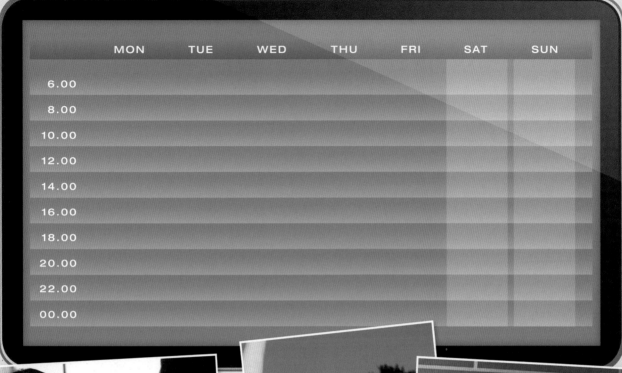

	MON	TUE	WED	THU	FRI	SAT	SUN
6.00							
8.00							
10.00							
12.00							
14.00							
16.00							
18.00							
20.00							
22.00							
00.00							

HOW TO SAY IT

Talking about routines

Are you free on Monday morning / Tuesday evening?

What about … ?

I'm free from … o'clock to … o'clock on Monday.

Do you work on Saturdays/Sundays?

No, I'm free all day on …

A For each day, tick (✓) the times when you are free. With a partner, compare your routines. Who has more free time?

A: *Are you free on Monday morning?*
B: *No, I'm not.*
A: *What about Monday evening?*
B: *Yes, I'm free then.*
A: *Great, what time?*
B: *At about seven.*

A 🎧 14 **LANGUAGE IN CONTEXT Listen to the conversation below. What does May's brother buy?**

Jake: Wow! Your brother has a lot of albums on his computer.

May: Yes, he does. He goes online and buys MP3s. He buys a new album every week! My sister likes music, too, but she doesn't buy MP3s. She buys CDs. She has hundreds. What about your sister? Does she like music?

Jake: No, she doesn't really like music, but she loves films. She often watches films online. I prefer music though. What about you?

May: Yes, me too.

Jake: Do you like this song?

May: Yes, I do.

Jake: Me, too! Let's listen to it!

NOTICE!

1 <u>Underline</u> all verbs in the conversation in the present simple. How many are there?

2 Is this conversation about general facts and habits or only about the present situation?

B **ANALYSE Read the conversation in Exercise A again.**

Form Complete the table with words from the conversation.

Affirmative	Negative	Yes/No questions	Short answers
I/You/We/They buy CDs.	I/You/We/They don't buy MP3s.	(3) _____ I/you/we/they like this song?	Yes, I/You/We/They (4) _____ .
He/She (1) _____ CDs. It sounds great.	He/She (2) _____ buy MP3s. It doesn't sound great.	Does he/she like music? Does it sound great?	Yes, he/she/it does. No, he/she/it doesn't.

Spelling rules

We usually make the form of the verb used with *he*, *she* or *it* by adding -*s* (e.g. *likes*). Also:

With verbs ending in …	we …
consonant + *y* (e.g. *study*)	replace *y* with -*ies* (e.g. *studies*)
s, sh, ch, z, x, o (e.g. *watch, fix, miss, go*)	add -*es* (e.g. *watches, fixes, misses, goes*)

WHAT'S RIGHT?
- ○ Do you like music? Yes, I like.
- ◐ Do you like music? Yes, I do.

WHAT'S RIGHT?
- ○ He like music.
- ◐ He likes music.

Function Tick (✓) the correct answers.

We use the present simple to talk about …
- ☐ general facts.
- ☐ feelings and states.
- ☐ things happening right now.
- ☐ routines and habits.

C **PRACTISE Complete the sentences with the correct form of the verbs in brackets.**

1 Charlie _____ (*like*) jazz music.
2 My brother and I _____ (*collect*) stamps.
3 Alison _____ planes at the weekend. (*fly*)
4 My brother _____ a lot of sport on TV. (*watch*)
5 _____ Sara and Kathy _____ (*listen*) to hip-hop?
6 Olivia _____ piano in her spare time. (*teach*)
7 _____ Richard _____ (*play*) the guitar?
8 My sister _____ (*not buy*) a lot of music.

D 🎤 **NOW YOU DO IT Work in pairs. Ask and answer questions about these things.**

hip-hop   stamps   a car   the piano

A: *Do you listen to hip-hop?*
B: *Yes, I do. How about you?*
A: *No, I don't.*

HOW TO SAY IT 🎤

Asking about habits
Do you listen to …?   *Do you play …?*
Do you collect …?   *Do you drive …?*

PRONUNCIATION: third person -s

A 🎧 15 Listen to the three sounds in the table below. Then listen to the words in the box, paying attention to the sound at the end of each of them. Write each one in the correct place in the table.

/s/	/z/	/ɪz/

listens practises plays wants relaxes
does likes watches collects

B 🗣️ 🎧 16 Work in pairs. Practise saying these sentences. Listen and check.

1 My dad listens to the radio every morning.
2 Jason practises the piano after school.
3 Mum likes walking the dog.
4 Our class sometimes watches English films.

READING: recognising cognates page 10 ⚙️

In English, long words that look difficult are often cognates in other languages. Look at long words carefully. You can often understand what the word means even if you recognise only part of it.

A Read this text. Find all the words which are similar to words in your language. Compare the words you find with a partner.

Do you want a celebrity hobby?

Celebrities have free time – and they have money! So what hobbies do they have, and can you do the same thing?

ACTOR: Tom Hanks
collects old typewriters!
Junk shops occasionally have antique typewriters. Or maybe your grandparents have a vintage one in the loft! Ask around. Look for ones that still work, or maybe that you can repair and maintain.

FILM DIRECTOR:
Quentin Tarantino
has a collection of old board games from TV shows!
Board games are not usually valuable unless they're in perfect condition. Like Tarantino, try to choose a theme – comic superhero games, or games based on films, for example.

ACTOR: Mila Kunis
plays the online computer game World of Warcraft!
Online players sometimes make life difficult for 'newbies'. Before you go online, practise playing similar computer games. When you are confident, connect to the internet and have a go. Don't be surprised when you die – a lot!

B Match each celebrity to the correct photo.

1 Tom Hanks
2 Quentin Tarantino
3 Mila Kunis

A

B

C

A 🎧 **17** Listen to the radio show. Choose the name for each statement.

1 Angelica / Victor likes sports games.
2 Angelica / Victor prefers action games.
3 Angelica / Victor doesn't like puzzle games.
4 Angelica / Victor plays driving games.

B 🗣 Work in groups. Discuss these questions.

| YES | ← | Do you play video games? | → | NO |

What video games do you play?
What's your favourite game? Why?
What video games don't you like?

What other games do you play?
Do you watch or play sports?
What's your favourite sport? Why?

A Tick (✓) the free-time activities you do once a week or more. How much time do you spend on each one in a typical week?

listen to music ☐ ———— hours

watch TV ☐ ———— hours

go online ☐ ———— hours

play sport ☐ ———— hours

see friends ☐ ———— hours

go bowling ☐ ———— hours

do exercise ☐ ———— hours

play video games ☐ ———— hours

go to the cinema ☐ ———— hours

B 🗣 Work in pairs. Compare your free-time activities. Who prefers doing things with other people? Who prefers doing things alone?

I listen to music for about five hours a week.

A LANGUAGE IN CONTEXT Read the information.
Answer the questions.

WE WANT TO MAKE A TV SHOW
ABOUT REAL FANS!

Are you a TV fan?

Tell us about the TV shows you watch.

What do you watch every day?

When do you watch them?

Why do you like them?

Where do you watch TV?

Who do you like to watch on TV?

Tell us and you can
be the next TV star!

NOTICE!
Underline all the question
words at the start of the
questions in the ad. What
verb follows the question
words?

баски ? gуши са в нас

B ANALYSE Read the ad in Exercise A again.

Form **Complete the table with one word from the ad.**

Question word	Auxiliary	Subject	Verb	
What/Where/When/Why/Who	_____	I/you/we/they	watch	
			do	...?
	does	he/she/it	go	

WHAT'S RIGHT?
- ✓ Where do you go in your free time?
- ○ Where you go in your free time?

Function **Choose the correct option to complete the sentence.**
We use questions beginning with *Wh-* question words to ...
a) find out information about people, places, times, etc.
b) check someone understands what we say.

C PRACTISE Use the prompts below to write questions.

1 why / you like tennis?
_____

2 when / Tom go to the gym?
_____

3 where / they meet for coffee?
_____

4 what / you want to do this evening?
_____

5 who / go out with in your free time?
_____

6 what / Jane do in her free time?
_____

D 🔊 **NOW YOU DO IT** Work in pairs. Ask and
answer questions about your free-time activities.
Are they similar or different?

HOW TO SAY IT 🔊
Talking about free-time activities.
What do you do in your free time?
Who do you play/go/watch ... with?
Why do you like it?
Because it's fun/interesting/exciting.

SPEAKING: asking for opinions

When you want to know what somebody thinks, you can use different phrases to ask for their opinion.

A 🎧 18 Listen to the conversation. What are they discussing?

B Listen to the conversation again. Tick (✓) the phrases you hear asking for opinions.

- ☐ And you?
- ☐ What's your opinion?
- ☐ Do you agree?
- ☐ What do you think?
- ☐ How about you?

C 🗣 Work in groups. Talk about your opinions of these kinds of films. Use phrases from Exercise B to ask about each other's opinions.

A: I like comedies. How about you?
B: No, I prefer action films.
A: Why?
B: Because comedies are silly. Action films are exciting.

science-fiction films

comedies

action films

love stories

VOCABULARY: personality adjectives

A 🗣 Tick (✓) A or B to complete this quiz. Calculate your score. Then compare with a partner.

Are you an ↓ *or an* ?

DO OUR QUIZ AND FIND OUT!

A		B	
1 I love parties.	○	1 I like quiet evenings at home.	◐
2 It's great to meet new people.	◉	2 I get nervous with people I don't know.	○
3 I like to talk … a lot!	○	3 I like being alone.	○
4 I hate being alone.	○	4 I prefer to listen rather than talk.	◉
5 I tell lots of jokes.	○	5 I've got a few close friends.	◐
6 I've got lots of friends.	○	6 I always help my friends when they need me.	◐
Number of As: _____		Number of Bs: _____	

B 🔊 Read about your personality type. Do you think what it says
is correct? Compare with a partner.

more As

You are an extrovert. You are **confident** and believe
in yourself. You don't get nervous easily. You are
sociable and love parties. You are **popular** and have
lots of friends. You are **funny** and you like telling jokes.

more Bs

You are an introvert. You are **shy** and are nervous
when you first meet people. You don't need other
people to have a good time and you're **independent**.
You never tell anyone your friends' secrets and you
are **loyal**. You are **considerate** and you care about
how other people feel.

C 🔊 Work in pairs. Think of someone you know well. Describe them to
your partner. Use the adjectives in **bold** from Exercise B.

My sister is an extrovert. She's very sociable. She likes …

WRITING: a personal description

A 🔊 How well do you know your classmates? Choose one person and
say three things you know about them.

B Read this webpage. What interests does Dimitri mention?

Who i am

Who I Am is the place to tell people about you,
your life, your interests, and to meet other people just like you!

| Home | My Profile | My Friends | My Link | Login |

Personal profile

Hi, everyone! I'm Dimitri Petukhov. I'm 23
years old and I live in an apartment with
two friends. I work in a large company and I
don't have a lot of free time in the week. In
the evenings, I watch TV or play video games
with my friends. At the weekends, I have
more time and I like running and playing
basketball. I also like going to the cinema.
My friends say I'm funny, and I agree! I think
I'm confident and love meeting new people.
I guess I'm an extrovert.

[Message] [Connect]

C Write about yourself for the website.
Describe your personality and your interests.

D Put your descriptions on the wall. Read your classmates'
descriptions. Find two people with interests similar to yours.

WHAT'S RIGHT?
○ I like listen to music.
○ I like listening to music.

LifeSkills

UNDERSTANDING YOUR LEARNING STYLE

- Identify your main learning style.
- Use it to help you learn new things.
- Try other styles to support your learning.

A Choose a new skill you want to learn. Say why.

play a musical instrument

learn a new sport

draw or paint

take amazing photos

juggle

speak a new language

B Tick (✓) your answers to complete this learning-style questionnaire. Calculate your scores.

LEARNING-STYLE QUESTIONNAIRE

1 How do you want to learn your new skill?
- ◆ in a class with other people
- ◇ by practising again and again
- ◆ by watching a DVD
- ◆ by reading a book about it

2 Think about learning English. How do you prefer to learn new words?
- ◆ I use the words in conversations.
- ◇ I act out the words.
- ◆ I draw pictures.
- ◆ I write the words.

3 How do you like to learn English grammar?
- ◆ by discussing it with my classmates
- ◇ by imagining myself in a situation
- ◆ by looking at diagrams
- ◆ by reading grammar rules

4 What do you do to remember someone's name?
- ◆ I use it in conversation with them.
- ◇ I say it over and over again.
- ◆ I make a mental picture of it.
- ◆ I write it down.

5 Which school activity do you prefer?
- ◆ debates and discussions
- ◇ sports and games
- ◆ art and design lessons
- ◆ reading and library work

Total number of
◆ _____
◇ _____
◆ _____
◆ _____

What is your first colour? _____

C Work in pairs. Follow these instructions to learn the words using your preferred learning style.

- Student A, look at the first group of words. Student B, look at the second group.
- Check the definitions of the words and phrases in a dictionary or ask your teacher.
- Read the instructions below that match your main colour from Exercise B.
- Follow the instructions to learn the words. You have five minutes.

Student A
- satellite dish
- current affairs
- broadcast

Student B
- lecture
- domain name
- tabloid

Interpersonal

Find another student to work with and talk about what the words mean.

Ask and answer questions using the words.

Test each other on the spelling and the meaning of the words.

Visual

Imagine each word in your mind.

Draw a picture to represent each word.

Try to remember each word and picture together.

Kinaesthetic

Imagine a situation where you need to use each word.

Do an action connected to that situation.

Try to remember each word and action together.

Linguistic

Write each word in a sentence and think of the definition.

Repeat each word a few times.

Try to remember each word and definition together.

D Work in pairs. Cover the words in Exercise C and test each other. How many words do you remember?

A: *Tell me one of the words.*
B: *The first word is …*
A: *What does it mean?*
B: *It means … What's the next word?*
A: *The next word is …*

E Look at your scores in Exercise B. What is your second colour? Use the instructions above to learn the new words/phrases below. After a few minutes, test each other. Which of the two ways of learning do you prefer?

puzzle pastime laid-back couch potato

REFLECT … How can the skill of understanding your learning style be useful to you in **Self and Society** and **Work and Career**?

Language wrap-up

1 VOCABULARY

A Rearrange the letters to make words to complete the sentences. (5 points)

1 I have a computer in my bedroom and I *og nenloi* _____ to buy music.
2 I *tlsine ot* _____ music every day. I love rap and hip-hop.
3 I *yalp ropts* _____ in my free time. I like football, but I prefer basketball.
4 I *ese inedfsr* _____ after school. We go bowling, go to the cinema or meet for coffee.
5 I *hatcw VT* _____ in the evening. I like reality shows and soap operas.

B Read about Anna and Katie. They are sisters, but they are very different. Match the adjectives to the explanations. (5 points)

1 Anna is very shy.   a) She makes everyone laugh with her jokes.
2 Katie is very funny.   b) She thinks about other people.
3 Anna is very considerate.   c) Her friends can trust her. She never says a bad thing about them.
4 Katie is very sociable.   d) She loves parties and being with a lot of friends.
5 Anna is very loyal.   e) She doesn't like meeting new people.

8 – 10 correct: I can talk about free-time activities and about people's personalities.
0 – 7 correct: Look again at the Vocabulary sections on pages 36 and 38.
SCORE: /10

2 GRAMMAR

Mark and Jodie are at Beth's party. Complete the conversation with the verbs in brackets in the present simple. (10 points)

Mark: Hi, I'm Mark.

Jodie: Oh, hi. I'm Jodie. So, how (1) _____ you _____ (know) Beth?

Mark: She (2) _____ (play) volleyball with my sister.

Jodie: Oh, cool. What (3) _____ you _____ (do), Mark?

Mark: I'm at university. I (4) _____ (study) French and German. And what about you?

Jodie: I (5) _____ (work) with my dad. He (6) _____ (have) a restaurant.

Mark: Oh, yeah? (7) _____ you _____ (like) it?

Jodie: It's OK, but I (8) _____ (not want) to do it my whole life.
        My mum (9) _____ (not think) it's a good job.

Mark: Oh, really? What (10) _____ she _____ (want) you to do?

Jodie: She wants me to be a doctor.

8 – 10 correct: I can use the present simple to talk about myself and to ask questions about other people.
0 – 7 correct: Look again at the Grammar sections on pages 34 and 37.
SCORE: /10

WRITING WORKSHOP

writing a personal
description

A Read the personal description and answer the questions.

Welcome to *You're the One!*

You're the One is a new reality TV show. Do you want to be on *You're the One?* Just tell us about yourself! Tell us about your life and your interests and be the next contestant on the new hit reality show *You're the One!*

Name: Olivia Best   Age: 19

Tell us about yourself!

Hi! I'm Olivia, and I want to be on *You're the One!* I live in Southampton with my parents, and I love going out! During the day, I work in an office, but at night I'm a party animal! I like listening to music and chatting to my friends. I'm popular and I've got a great sense of humour. My friends say I'm crazy, but I'm also sensitive and caring. I love the outdoor life and romantic evenings in front of a fire!

SUBMIT

1 Who is this personal description from? _____
2 What does she want to do? _____
3 What words does she use to describe herself? _____

B Look at the personal description again and choose the correct answers.

1 Who is the target reader for this personal description?
   a) someone who likes reality TV   b) someone who works for a TV company
2 What style does the writer use?
   a) a fun, chatty style   b) a serious, academic style
3 What punctuation does the writer use to make it lively?
   a) question marks (?)   b) exclamation marks (!)
4 What tense does the writer use to talk about facts and habits?
   a) present continuous   b) present simple

C Match the adjectives to the definitions. If necessary, work with a partner and use a dictionary.

If you are …

1 caring,   a) you do fun, mad things that your friends love!
2 crazy,   b) you love meeting new people and making friends.
3 lively,   c) your feelings get hurt easily.
4 outgoing,   d) you think about other people's feelings.
5 romantic,   e) you think love is important.
6 sensitive,   f) you are full of energy and never stop!

D NOW YOU DO IT Imagine you want to be on *You're the One*.
Write a personal description to apply for the show.

HOW ARE YOU DOING?

Look back at your writing and tick the statements that are true.
- ◯ The style is fun and chatty.
- ◯ There are exclamation marks to make my writing lively.
- ◯ The present simple describes facts about me and my life.
- ◯ The description is clear and interesting.

Now ask a partner to look at your writing and tick. Is the personal description clear and interesting?
- ● Well done!
- ◐ Nearly! Look at the unit again.
- ● Think again! Ask your teacher for help.

Down time   **UNIT 3**   **43**

UNIT 4 DAY IN, DAY OUT

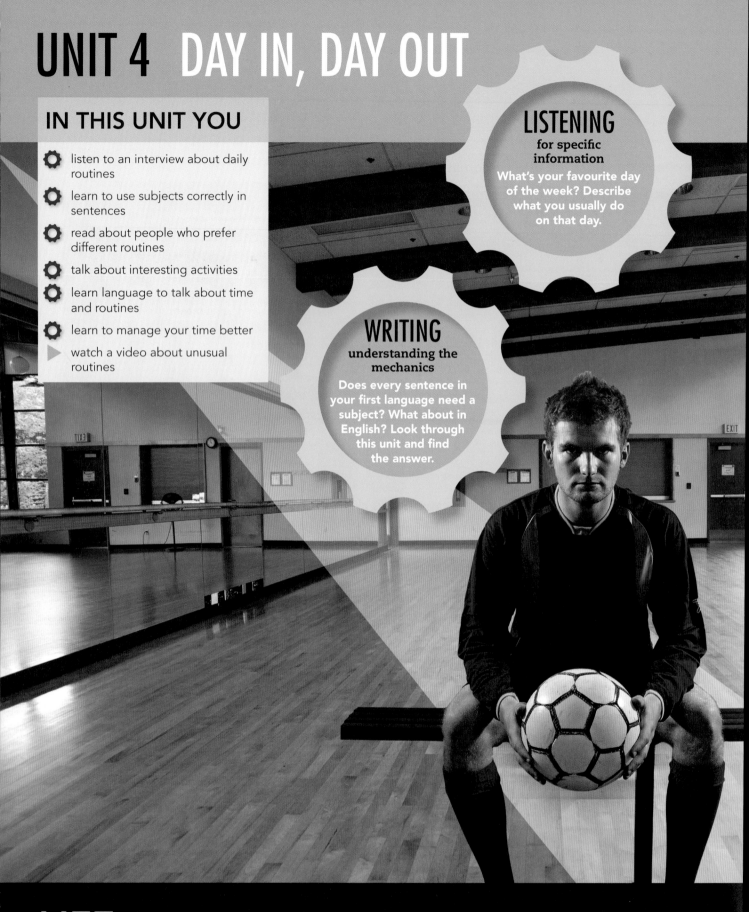

IN THIS UNIT YOU

- listen to an interview about daily routines
- learn to use subjects correctly in sentences
- read about people who prefer different routines
- talk about interesting activities
- learn language to talk about time and routines
- learn to manage your time better
- watch a video about unusual routines

LISTENING
for specific information
What's your favourite day of the week? Describe what you usually do on that day.

WRITING
understanding the mechanics
Does every sentence in your first language need a subject? What about in English? Look through this unit and find the answer.

LIFE SKILLS
SELF & SOCIETY

managing your time Say what you do to remember the things you have to do. Do you write them down / remember them in your head / do something else?

A Read these sayings about time. With a partner, discuss what you think each one means.

A: *So, what do you think the first one means?*
B: *Maybe it means that time never stops. Or that no one can stop time.*
A: *Yes, I think you're right.*

Time waits for no man.

Don't put off until tomorrow what you can do today.

Time flies when you are having fun.

Life's too short to worry.

The early bird catches the worm.

B Work in pairs. Do you agree with the sayings in Exercise A?

A Match these sentences to the correct times. Some times match more than one sentence.

midday/noon = 12.00 in the day	
midnight = 12.00 at night	
am = before midday, e.g. 7am	
pm = after midday, e.g. 11pm	

1	It's twenty past seven.	4	It's quarter past two.	7	It's seven twenty.	10	It's five forty-five.
2	It's five to two.	5	It's six thirty.	8	It's half past six.		
3	It's three o'clock.	6	It's quarter to six.	9	It's two fifteen.		

B Work in pairs. Say what time you usually do these things on weekdays.

- get up
- leave for university/work
- get to university/work
- have lunch
- have dinner
- go to bed

A: *What time do you have lunch?*
B: *I have lunch at (about) two. And you?*

A Read this article. What is the difference between larks and owls?

What Type of **Bird** *Are You?*

One in ten people is a lark. About two in ten are owls and enjoy staying up very late. If you like to get up early, have coffee and read the paper, you're probably a lark. Owls often don't eat breakfast and have to hurry to get to work in the morning. If you do your washing or surf the internet at midnight, you're probably an owl.

Larks and owls often have different jobs. A & E doctors, for example, work more at night. They are usually owls. Writers and artists are often larks. For example, cartoonist Scott Adams is a lark. 'I never try to do any creating past noon,' he says. 'And I only exercise in the late afternoon. I draw from 6am to 7am. Then I write for a few hours.'

Larks
- best before noon
- go to bed early
- favourite meal: breakfast
- drink coffee in the morning

Owls
- best after 6pm
- stay up late
- favourite meal: dinner
- drink coffee in the evening

B Work in pairs. Ask and answer these questions.

1 Are you a lark or an owl? Why?
2 What time of day do you like to work or study?
3 What time of day do you like to relax?

A 🎧 **19 LANGUAGE IN CONTEXT** Listen to the conversation below. Answer the questions.

Rick: I'm **always** so busy! I **never** have any free time. I'm **usually** at work in the morning and I **always** study in the afternoon. What about you?

Alicia: I don't work, so I **often** get up late. I **sometimes** study in the morning and I relax in the afternoon. **Five times a week**, I go out with my friends.

Rick: Five times a week! I **rarely** have time to go out – maybe just **once a month**. But I love watching films. How often do you go to the cinema?

Alicia: Oh, **three or four times a month**. Do you want to go this weekend?

Rick: Yeah, that sounds great.

1 Who does a lot every day? _____
2 Who doesn't do a lot every day? _____

B ANALYSE Read the conversation in Exercise A again.

Form Choose the correct option to complete the sentences.

1 The adverbs of frequency in bold come _____ the verb *be*.
   a) before   b) after
2 The adverbs of frequency in bold come _____ other verbs.
   a) before   b) after
3 The adverbial phrases (*once a month*, etc) come _____.
   a) at the start or end of a clause   b) between subject and verb

Function Complete the diagram with two words from the conversation.

We use adverbs of frequency to talk about **how often** something happens

0% ←——————————————————→ 100%

never _____ sometimes often usually _____

NOTICE!

Look at the underlined phrases in the conversation. Is the word order
a) the same?
b) different?

WHAT'S RIGHT?
○ I am always happy.
○ I always am happy.

C PRACTISE Write sentences about how often Rick does each of these activities. Use each frequency adverb from Exercise B once.

be late for class	0 times a week	(1) *He is never late for class*
cook at home	6 times a week	(2) _____
chat online	3 times a month	(3) _____
drive to work	every workday	(4) _____
play video games	once a year	(5) _____
watch the news	4 times a week	(6) _____

D 🗣 **NOW YOU DO IT** Work in groups. Ask and answer questions to find out how often people in your group do each activity in Exercise C. Then report back to the whole class.

A: In our group, Victor and Lisa rarely cook at home.
B: Vera always cooks at home.

HOW TO SAY IT 🗣

Asking about frequency
How often do you …?
How often are you …?

A 📻 **20** Listen to the names of the days of the week and (circle) the stressed syllable. Then listen again and repeat.

Mon–day   Tues–day   Wednes–day   Thurs–day   Fri–day   Sat–ur–day   Sun–day

B 📻 **21** Work in pairs. Practise saying these sentences. Make sure you stress the correct syllable. Listen and check.

1   I work from Monday to Friday.
2   I go to the gym on Tuesdays and Wednesdays.
3   My favourite day of the week is Saturday.
4   I think Sundays are boring.

LISTENING: for specific information page 24 ⚙

A 📻 **22** Look at the photos and listen to Part 1 of an interview. Match each photo to the day the woman does the activity.

_____ Monday   _____ Thursday
_____ Tuesday   _____ Friday
_____ Wednesday   _____ Saturday

B 📻 **23** Listen to Part 2 of the interview. What does the woman do on Sundays? Tick (✓) the activities she mentions.

☐ have breakfast   ☐ have lunch
☐ read the newspaper   ☐ do the housework
☐ watch TV   ☐ go to the gym
☐ go for a walk   ☐ cook
☐ meet friends

C 🗣 Work in pairs. Describe your usual weekend routine. Do you and your partner do similar or different things on weekends?

On Saturdays, I usually get up late. I ...

on Mondays = every Monday

VOCABULARY prepositions of time

A Read what this woman says about her routine. Choose the correct option to complete the sentences.

'I usually work until five o'clock. I get home at six. On weekdays, I go to bed early. I often watch TV until bedtime. On Fridays, I always go out after work. I see friends in the evenings. Sometimes, I don't get home before 3am! I sleep in on Saturday mornings.'

1   We use until / before / after to say when we stop doing something.
2   We use until / before / after to say at a later time.
3   We use until / before / after to say at an earlier time.

B Read the text in Exercise A again. Write two more examples of your own for each category in the table below.

on	at	in	before	after	until
Fridays	five	the evening	3am	work	bedtime

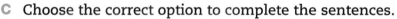

C Choose the correct option to complete the sentences.

1   My English class starts _____ two thirty.
    a) in   b) until   c) at
2   Let's go out _____ Thursday.
    a) in   b) on   c) at
3   I always brush my teeth _____ I have a shower.
    a) until   b) before   c) at

4   I study _____ about 10pm, and then I go to bed.
    a) after   b) at   c) until
5   See you _____ the morning!
    a) on   b) in   c) at
6   My dad usually plays tennis _____ work.
    a) on   b) until   c) after

SPEAKING: talking about interesting activities

A))24 Listen to the conversation below. Answer the questions.

Eve: So, Owen, what do you do when you're not at university?
Owen: I usually have a very busy week. I do different activities almost every evening.
Eve: Really? What activities do you do?
Owen: Well, I go in-line skating twice a week. And I have an art class on Wednesday evenings.
Eve: An art class? That's interesting!
Owen: Why don't you come along next week?
Eve: Sounds fun. And what do you usually do at the weekend?
Owen: I go hang-gliding on Saturday. Do you want to come along to try that?
Eve: No way! Art class is exciting enough for me!

1   What activity does Owen do twice a week? _____
2   What activity is Eve interested in trying? _____

B Walk around the class and ask each person to tell you two interesting or unusual things they do each week. Find out as much as you can.

A: *Do you do anything unusual each week?*
B: *On Tuesdays, I go to a dance class.*

C Tell the rest of the class about any interesting or unusual things your classmates do.

GRAMMAR: clauses with *until, before, after*

A LANGUAGE IN CONTEXT Read what this man says and choose T (true) or F (false).

'I'm pretty superstitious. I stay in the dressing room until I'm the last one. Then I follow the others. I always touch the grass before I start to play. It brings me luck. After I do all of that, I always play well!'

1 He is the last one in the dressing room then he follows the others. T / F

2 He starts to play, then touches the grass. T / F

B ANALYSE Read the text in Exercise A again.

Function Choose the correct option to complete the sentences.

> **NOTICE!**
>
> <u>Underline</u> **after**, **before** and **until** in the text. They come _____
>
> **a)** between clauses or at the start of a clause
>
> **b)** between the subject and the verb

To talk about the order of events …

after	After I do all of that, I always play well.	We use *after* with the **(1)** first / second event.
before	I always touch the grass before I start to play.	We use *before* with the **(2)** first / second event.

To talk about the duration of events …

until	I stay in the dressing room until I'm the last one.	We use *until* to talk about an event that stops at a particular moment in time.

C PRACTISE Complete these sentences with *before*, *after* or *until*.

1 Dan has his piano lesson at seven. He has dinner at nine.
Dan has his piano lesson _____ he has dinner.
Dan has dinner _____ he has his piano lesson.

2 I get home. Then I call my friends.
I call my friends _____ I get home.

3 Christina studies every day. She stops when she finishes all her school work.
Christina studies every day _____ she finishes all her school work.

4 I arrive at the office. Then I have coffee.
I have coffee _____ I arrive at the office.
I arrive at the office _____ I have coffee.

> **WHAT'S RIGHT?**
> ○ I get dressed before I have breakfast.
> ○ I get dressed before have breakfast.

D **NOW YOU DO IT** Work in pairs. Ask and answer questions about what you do before and after you do these things.

* leave the house in the morning
* do your homework
* go out in the evening with friends
* go to bed

A: *What do you do before you leave the house in the morning?*
Before I leave the house in the morning, I …

A sentence expresses a whole idea. Sentences in English always have a subject and a verb. When there is no other subject, we use *it*.

A Tick (✓) the correct sentences. Rewrite the incorrect sentences.

1 ☐ Friday my favourite day. _____
2 ☐ It is twenty to seven. _____
3 ☐ Is cold today. _____
4 ☐ I an unusual routine. _____
5 ☐ My dad gets up at 4am. _____
6 ☐ Is an interesting job. _____

B Read about an unusual routine. Find three sentences that are incorrect and <u>underline</u> them. Explain why they are incorrect and suggest changes.

The life of a roadie isn't easy! And Jake Redman knows. This is his tenth year as a roadie with some of the biggest names in music. He has a hard routine on tour. He get up at midday when the tour bus arrives at the next stadium. He starts work straight away – he helps to get the stadium ready for the show. It takes four hours and fifty people! Is hard work. Then, it's time for a meal and a little free time. Sometimes he watches the show in the evening. When the show is over, after midnight, goes back to work. He puts all the equipment away and finally gets to sleep at around four in the morning. What a life!

C Think of someone (a member of your family, a celebrity, etc) with an unusual routine. Write a few sentences in your notebook describing what you think he/she does on a typical day.

D 🔊 Work in pairs. Read each other's sentences. Do the two people have similar or different routines?

E 🔊 Read your partner's sentences again. Is every sentence correct? Help your partner find any mistakes.

LifeSkills

MANAGING YOUR TIME

- Understand any problems you have with managing your time.
- Write a to-do list and categorise each task.
- Decide on the best order for the tasks.

A How well do you manage your time? Complete this quiz. Compare your answers in pairs. How accurate is the quiz? What can you do to improve your time management?

IT'S TIME TO THINK ABOUT TIME!

Some of us are born to be late and others are always on time. Take our fun quiz to find out which you are!

1 How do you feel about time?
- a) I never have enough time!
- b) Sometimes I don't have time to do everything, but usually it's OK.
- c) Time? I have lots of it!

2 Do you arrive on time for things?
- a) Yes, always.
- b) Sometimes, but not always.
- c) No, I'm always late!

3 Do you often have nothing to do?
- a) No, I'm always busy.
- b) Sometimes.
- c) Yes, I do.

4 How often do you check the time?
- a) I'm too busy to look at the clock!
- b) Never. I don't have a watch.
- c) Often. I like to know what time it is.

5 You have something important to do. How do you feel?
- a) I'm not worried because there's lots of time.
- b) Help! I have a thousand things to do today!
- c) Forget it. I can do it tomorrow.

6 How do you work or study?
- a) I just work until I finish.
- b) I take lots of breaks to watch TV and chat online.
- c) It's difficult! I never have time to finish my work or study.

Now add up your score:
1. a 3   b 2   c 1
2. a 1   b 2   c 3
3. a 3   b 2   c 1
4. a 3   b 1   c 2
5. a 2   b 3   c 1
6. a 2   b 1   c 3

My total _____

6–10
You have a lot of time – because you don't do important things! Manage your time better and you can achieve more.

11–15
You have a good attitude towards time. With a little time management, you can do even more.

16–18
You need to manage your time and give yourself time to relax!

B Make a list of things to do in the coming week. Estimate the time you need for each one. Look at this example.

To-do list

DAY: Monday

do the washing	2 hours
go to the bank	1 hour
go to the cinema	3 hours

C 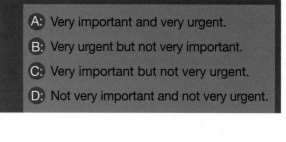 Work in pairs. Ask and answer questions about your lists. Use the diagram and mark each task depending on how important and how urgent it is.

Key to diagram:

A: Very important and very urgent.

B: Very urgent but not very important.

C: Very important but not very urgent.

D: Not very important and not very urgent.

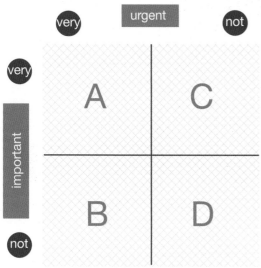

HOW TO SAY IT

Prioritising

Is this urgent?

How important is this?

It's very important!

I don't really need to …

I suppose this isn't really urgent, so …

D Write your things to do in order. For each day of the week, write A things first, followed by B things, etc. Think about the time you have and consider moving some things from one day to another.

Monday	
Tuesday	
Wednesday	
Thursday	
Friday	
Saturday	
Sunday	

E 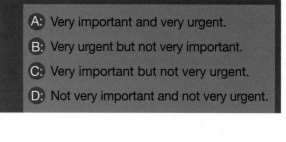 Work in pairs. Compare your daily to-do lists. Can you do everything in the time you have?

 REFLECT … How can the skill of managing your time be useful to you in **Work and Career** and **Study and Learning**?

Language wrap-up

1 VOCABULARY

A Rita is talking about her day. Look at the time on each watch. Then complete these sentences with a verb and the correct time. (6 points)

1 I _____ to school at _____.   2 I _____ dinner at _____.   3 I _____ to bed at _____.

B Rita is talking about other parts of her day. Choose the correct prepositions to complete the sentences. (4 points)

1 I always have breakfast at / before / after / until I go to school.
2 I sometimes go for coffee with friends until / at / after / on school.
3 On / In / Until / At Saturday nights, I use my computer or watch a film
   before / after / on / until midnight and then I go to bed.

> **8 – 10 correct:** I can tell the time and use prepositions to talk about what I do in a typical day.
> **0 – 7 correct:** Look again at the Vocabulary sections on pages 46 and 49.
> **SCORE:**   /10

2 GRAMMAR

A Read this text about how frequently five people play video games. Write their names in the correct order on the scale. (5 points)

When Leo comes home from school, he always plays video games. His sister, Marina, sometimes plays with him, but she prefers going online to chat to her friends. David often plays video games after school, but not every day. His sister, Lola, never plays. She thinks video games are boring. Samuel rarely plays video games, but he likes one football game that he plays with his brother.

100% ← _____ → 0%

1 _____   2 _____   3 _____   4 _____   5 _____

B Rewrite the sentences with *before*, *after* or *until*. Use the correct punctuation. (5 points)

1 Leo has dinner and then he plays games on his computer.
   _____ (*before*)
2 Marina chats to friends online. She stops when it's time for bed.
   _____ (*until*)
3 David does his homework. Then he plays video games.
   _____ (*after*)
4 Lola watches TV. She stops when she goes to bed.
   _____ (*until*)
5 Samuel plays a video game and then he listens to music.
   _____ (*after*)

> **8 – 10 correct:** I can use adverbs of frequency and time clauses to talk about when and how often people do things.
> **0 – 7 correct:** Look again at the Grammar sections on pages 47 and 50.
> **SCORE:**   /10

SPEAKING WORKSHOP

A **Read the interview. Complete the interview with the questions below.**

Mark: Now, this week the show is about interesting hobbies. With me today I've got Annie. Hello, Annie.

Annie: Hi. It's good to be here.

Mark: You've got a very interesting hobby. (1) _____

Annie: OK. I go flyboarding.

Mark: (2) _____

Annie: It's a hobby where you stand on a kind of skateboard on water. Powerful jets of water push you into the air. In the air, you fly around and do tricks.

Mark: (3) _____

Annie: You dive into and out of the water like a dolphin! You also do jumps and loops in the air.

Mark: (4) _____

Annie: Oh, yes. Of course. You have to check your equipment before you start. Never start until you're sure everything is safe. And you need someone to help you with the jets of water.

Mark: (5) _____

Annie: Once a week. I live near a lake, so I go every Saturday.

Mark: (6) _____

Annie: Yes, definitely! It's a lot of fun!

Mark: Annie, thank you for talking to us today.

Annie: My pleasure!

a) **Can you tell us more about** the tricks?
b) Would you recommend it to other people?
c) **Why don't you tell us** what you do?
d) **How often do you** go flyboarding?
e) **What is that exactly?**
f) **Do you think** safety is important?

B **Look at the phrases in bold in the interview questions. Match each phrase to its function below.**

We use this phrase to …
1 ask about frequency.   _____
2 ask someone's opinion.   _____
3 ask someone to start describing something.   _____
4 ask someone to explain something in detail.   _____
5 ask for further information about something.   _____

C **Work in pairs. Imagine you have an unusual hobby (e.g. bungee-jumping, sky-diving) and you are on a radio show to talk about it. Roleplay an interview with your partner.**

Things to include:
• questions about the activity
• interesting descriptions and details about the activity

D **Now find a new partner and roleplay the interview again. Try to remember to include things from the list in Exercise C.**

HOW ARE YOU DOING?

Think about your speaking. Do you feel confident …
○ asking and answering questions about an activity?
○ asking for and giving further details about the activity?
○ asking for and giving opinions and recommendations?
How do you feel about your speaking generally?
● ○ ●
Very confident   Not sure …   Need to practise

UNIT 5 HERE, THERE AND EVERYWHERE

IN THIS UNIT YOU

- learn language for talking about places
- read descriptions of where people live
- give and ask for directions to places in your town
- listen to a news report describing a festival in a city
- write emails giving and asking for directions
- make suggestions to a visitor to your town
- ▶ watch a video about an interesting festival

SPEAKING
checking understanding
When should you check that you understand everything someone is saying? What are people checking in this unit?

READING
for the main idea
Where do you often see written opinions? Do you often read people's opinions? Why or why not?

LIFE SKILLS
SELF & SOCIETY

establishing priorities In what situations do you need to order things according to how important they are? Are you good at this? Why or why not?

HOW TO SAY IT

Expressing opinions

I think it's in … because there is/are …

It's probably …

I don't think it's…

I would like to attend the … because I like …

A Look at the photos. Where do you think each of these events is happening? Give reasons for your answers. Which of these events would you like to attend? Why?

B Work in groups. Talk about your favourite things to do and places to visit.

A: *I really like London.*

B: *Me too! I love going to all the museums.*

GRAMMAR: *there is / there are* with *some, any, several, a lot of, many*

A **LANGUAGE IN CONTEXT** Read about the UFO festival. Answer the questions.

Helen:
'I'm from Canada, and I'm travelling in the southwest USA. Are there any interesting festivals in this area this month? Is there a festival in Arizona? I'm in Phoenix at the moment.'

Jan:
'There aren't any festivals in Arizona this month, but there is a great festival in Roswell, New Mexico. It's called the UFO Festival, and it's all about UFOs and aliens! There are a lot of different types of events. For example, there are several planetarium shows and there are some talks by astronomers and other scientists. There aren't many tickets for these talks, so it's a good idea to buy them online as soon as possible. There's an alien costume competition, and there are many contestants with really crazy costumes! There's also an alien parade. Believe me, there isn't another festival like the UFO Festival!'

1   Where is the UFO Festival?
2   What types of events does the festival include?
3   Are all the events in the festival free?

B **ANALYSE** Read the text in Exercise A again.

NOTICE!

1   The writers use the phrases **there is / there are / there aren't / are there**. Do these phrases refer to things or actions? _____

2   How do we form a contraction of **there is**? _____

Function **Choose the correct options to complete the sentences.**
1   We use *there is / there are* to …
    a)   say that something exists.   b)   indicate the location of something.
2   We use words like *some, any* and *several* to talk about …
    a)   exact quantities.   b)   general quantities.

Form **Complete the sentences in the table with the correct form of *there is / there are*.**

Affirmative	
_____	a great festival in Roswell, New Mexico.
_____	an alien costume competition.
_____	a lot of different types of events.
_____	several planetarium shows.
_____	some talks by astronomers and other scientists.
Negative	
_____	another festival like the UFO Festival!
_____	any festivals in Arizona this month.
_____	many tickets for these talks.
Questions	
_____	a festival in Arizona?
_____	any interesting festivals in this area this month?

WHAT'S RIGHT?
◯ There are a lot of people.
◯ There is a lot of people.

C **PRACTISE** Choose the correct options to complete the sentences.

1   There isn't / aren't any festivals in my country in November.
2   Is / Are there any food festivals in your town?
3   In Venice, there is / are a carnival in February.
4   There are several / any carnivals around the world every year.
5   Are there any / a dance competitions during the festival?
6   There is / are a lot of people in the parade.
7   There isn't a / some festival like the UFO Festival in my country.
8   There are any / a lot of festivals in the summer.

D **NOW YOU DO IT** Work in pairs. Choose a festival in your city or country. Describe it for your partner to guess. Then switch roles.

A: *It's in August. There are musicians. There's a parade.*
B: *The music festival!*

A »)🎧 25 Listen to the message about the Chinese New Year festival. Circle the places on the map that the speaker mentions.

Chinese New Year
festival **and** *parade*

It's time for the Chinese New Year!
Come and join the celebrations.
The colourful dragon parade covers
the following route this year:

zoo

science museum

chocolate factory

main square

fountain

start bus station

cinema

art gallery

park

end point

shopping centre

B 🗣 Work in pairs. Answer the questions.

1 How many places on the map are also in your town?
  A: *There's a zoo.*
  B: *Yes, and there are several …*
2 How many other places in your town can you name in English?
  A: *There are a lot of banks.*
  B: *And there's a history museum.*

PRONUNCIATION: compound nouns

A »)🎧 26 Listen to the compound nouns (noun + noun). Underline the stressed word in each pair.

science museum   shopping centre   chocolate factory   art gallery

In compound nouns, do we stress the first word or the second word? _____

B 🗣 Work in pairs. Make new compound nouns for places in your city. Then practise saying the words.

1 history museum   2 train station   3 car factory
   _____ museum   _____ station   _____ factory

C 🗣 Work in pairs. Use compound nouns from Exercises A and B, or think of others, and write sentences about things in your town. Practise reading your sentences.

There are two shopping centres here. There's a history museum and an art gallery.

Here, there and everywhere   UNIT 5   59

READING: for the main idea

When you read a text, think about these questions. What is the general topic? What is the writer saying about the topic?

A Read these texts quickly. Choose the main topic.

a) neighbourhoods   b) festivals   c) families

Emile

'I live in a quiet area in Paris. I like living there because it's very friendly and there are several shops and cafés. The only problem is that it's a bit boring sometimes because there aren't any clubs. There's a good stadium, though. I often go to sports events.'

'I live in Singapore, in a very busy neighbourhood. I don't like it because it's noisy and there's lots of traffic. There's a shopping centre near my house, and I go there a lot. There are also museums and a cinema in the area, but I don't have time to go to them. There's a good food festival in April, though.'

Melissa

Carlos

'I live in a nice neighbourhood in the city of Montevideo, Uruguay. The neighbourhood is pretty small, and a lot of our neighbours are my friends. There aren't many big shops near here, but there are some nice small shops. There's also an art gallery, a cinema, and a gym. Oh, and there are a lot of great restaurants! I think it's a fantastic place to live.'

B Read the texts in Exercise A again. Decide whether each person has a positive or negative opinion of where they live and choose the correct option.

Emile: positive / negative   **Melissa:** positive / negative   **Carlos:** positive / negative

C Work in pairs. Talk about your neighbourhood. Do you like it? Why or why not?

I like my neighbourhood because it's small and …

LISTENING: to a news report

A 27 Listen to the start of a news report. Choose the correct option to complete the sentences.

1 Buñol is near the city of …   a) Valencia.   b) Murcia.
2 *La Tomatina* festival happens in …   a) September.   b) August.

B 28 Listen to the rest of the report. Choose the correct option to complete the sentences.

1 Mary speaks to a man from …
   a) Spain.   b) Britain.   c) Germany.
2 All the people go to … to have breakfast.
   a) the main square   b) the park   c) their houses
3 At eleven o'clock, everyone …
   a) goes home.   b) throws tomatoes.   c) eats tomatoes.
4 The festival continues for …
   a) two weeks.   b) two days.   c) two hours.

C Give your opinion. What do you think about *La Tomatina* festival? What do you think about festivals in general? Give reasons.

I think they're fun.
I don't like them because there are always a lot of people!

GRAMMAR: the imperative

A 🔊 **29 LANGUAGE IN CONTEXT** Listen to this conversation.
Then choose the correct option to complete the sentences below.

Rick: Excuse me. Is there a cashpoint near here?

Martina: Yes, there's one in the Union Bank. It's on the High Street.

Rick: How do I get there?

Martina: <u>Go</u> straight ahead on this street for about 50 metres. <u>Turn</u> right at Park Street
           and <u>go</u> past the post office. Then <u>turn</u> left onto River Street and <u>walk</u> towards
           the main square. The bank is on the left, next to the supermarket.
           <u>Don't go</u> into the bank. The cashpoint is outside.

Rick: OK, right at Park Street, then left onto River Street.

Martina: That's right. <u>Don't worry</u>. It's easy to get there!

Rick: Thank you very much.

Martina: You're welcome.

1   Rick wants to …
    a)   get money.
    b)   buy something.
    c)   eat lunch.
2   Martina tells him …
    a)   the location of the bank.
    b)   directions to get there.
    c)   both.

NOTICE!

1   The <u>underlined</u> words in the
    conversation are
    a)   nouns.
    b)   verbs.
    c)   adjectives.
2   Martina uses these words to
    a)   give directions.
    b)   ask questions.
    c)   give personal information.

B   ANALYSE Read the conversation in Exercise A again.

Form **Read the examples in the table below and choose the correct option to complete the sentences. Then add one more example to each column of the table.**

Affirmative	Negative
Go straight ahead on this street.	Don't go into the bank.
Turn right onto Park Street.	Don't worry.
Walk about 50 metres.	Don't talk.
Read the signs.	Don't be late!
Please write your name.	

1   In the imperative form, there is / is not a subject before the base form of the verb.
2   Negative imperatives have don't / doesn't before the base form of the verb.

Function **Choose the correct option to complete the sentence.**
We use the imperative to talk about routines / give instructions or directions.

C   PRACTISE Put the words in order to make sentences.

1   Street / onto / turn / left / Baker

2   to / this / song / listen

3   instructions / read / the

4   at / don't / answers / the / look

5   for / concert / tickets / buy / the / two

6   book / don't / open / your

D 🗣 **NOW YOU DO IT** Work in small groups. Take turns giving and following
instructions.

Go straight ahead. Turn right. No, don't turn left; turn right. Stop.
Walk to the door. Open the door. Don't close it.
Close your book. Look at me.

A Read and match the sentences to the pictures.

1 Take the second street on the left.
2 Make a U-turn.
3 It's on Laurel Avenue.
4 It's next to the museum.
5 Follow the signs for the zoo.
6 It's opposite the cinema.

7 Turn left here.
8 Go over the bridge.
9 It's between the bank and the school.
10 Go straight ahead.
11 Take the first right.
12 It's on the corner of Mason Road and Laurel Avenue.

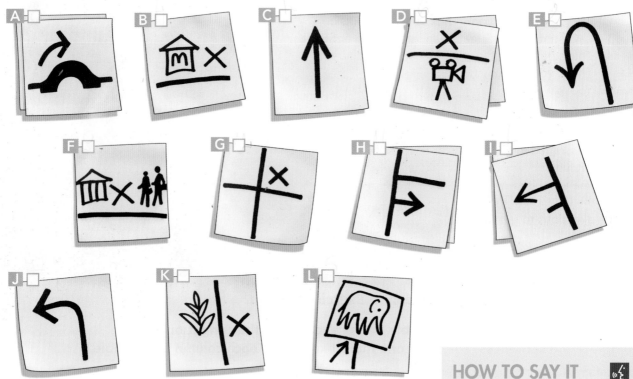

HOW TO SAY IT

Asking for and giving directions

Excuse me, where is the …?
How do I get to …?
Is there a … near here?
Turn left/right onto/at …

B Look at this street map. Student A, you are at the main square. Student B, you are at the art gallery. Ask each other for directions to different places on the map.

A: *How do I get to the zoo from here?*
B: *Turn right onto Main Street. Take the first street on the left. That's River Street. Then …*

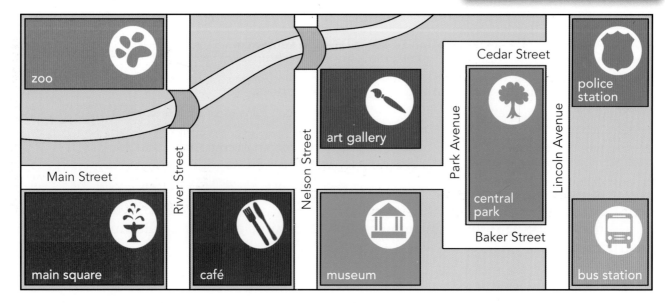

SPEAKING: repeating directions to check understanding

When you ask for directions, listen carefully and repeat the essential information to check that you understand.

A **30 Listen to the conversations below.**
<u>Underline</u> **the information that Speaker A repeats.**

1   A: Excuse me, how do I get to the main square?
    B: Take the first right, and go straight ahead. Then turn left onto Post Street.
    A: OK. First right, then left onto Post Street.
    B: That's right.
    A: Thank you.
    B: You're welcome.

2   A: Excuse me, is there a bank near here?
    B: Yes, there's one on Fort Street.
    A: Fort Street. OK. And how do I get there?
    B: Go straight ahead, and take the third left.
    A: Straight ahead, and take the second left.
    B: No, not the second left, the third left.
    A: Third left. OK, thanks.

B   **Work in pairs. Take turns asking for directions to places in your town.**

A: *Excuse me, how do I get from … to …?*
B: *Take the … It's on …*

WRITING: an email to give directions

A   **Read this email from a friend. What does Avril need?**

To: my_friend@mymail.mac.wd
From: avril_wright@mymail.mac.wd
Subject: Directions

Hi!
Thanks for inviting me to the exhibition. I don't know where the art gallery is, exactly. I need directions from the bus station to the gallery. How do I get there?
Thanks a lot!
Avril

HOW TO SAY IT

Giving directions
Hi, …
OK. Here are the directions to …
From …
Then …
Don't get lost!
See you soon!

B   **Look at the map on page 62 again. In your notebook, write an email to Avril giving her directions.**

LifeSkills

ESTABLISHING PRIORITIES

- Understand the criteria.
- List the options.
- Order the options according to the criteria.

A Read the comment below from a travel website.
Tick (✓) Danny's two main criteria.

a) He doesn't want to spend a lot of money. ☐ d) He doesn't want to visit a museum. ☐

b) He wants to go shopping. ☐ e) He wants to see as much as possible. ☐

c) He doesn't have a lot of time. ☐

i-TRAVEL ✈

The website for travel inspiration

⬚ GO

HOME

LOGIN

REGISTER

ABOUT i-TRAVEL

Posted on:
03/05/14 at 09:34
by Danny1992
Registered:
15/03/10
Posts: 5

Forum: one day in …

Subject: Where to go? Help!

I'm in the city for one day next week and I don't know what to visit. I arrive at 7.00 in the morning and leave on the 8pm bus. I haven't got much money – only £40. Please give me some ideas!

Thanks!

Replies: 0

REPLY   ◄ **PREVIOUS | NEXT** ►

B 🗣 Work in pairs. In your notebook, make a list of the main attractions in your city. Write down as many as you can. Then write the cost and the time you need to visit each one.

What?	How much?	How long?

HOW TO SAY IT 🗣

Talking about things to do

How long do you need to visit …?
I think you need … hours.
How much does the … cost?
I think it costs … dollars / pounds / euros.
I think it's free.

C Work in pairs. Complete this *Top 5 Things to Do!* list for Danny using your options from Exercise B. Decide why you think Danny should see or do these things. Remember to consider the amount of time and money he has.

Gregg's Chocolate Factory tour
Reason: It's cheap (only £12) and interesting

Top 5 Things To Do!

1.
Reason:
2.
Reason:
3.
Reason:
4.
Reason:
5.
Reason:

D Write a short response to Danny.

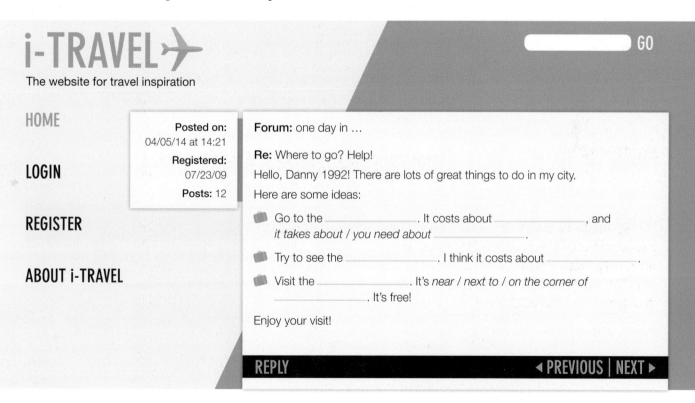

i-TRAVEL ✈

The website for travel inspiration

GO

HOME

LOGIN

REGISTER

ABOUT i-TRAVEL

Posted on:
04/05/14 at 14:21
Registered:
07/23/09
Posts: 12

Forum: one day in …

Re: Where to go? Help!

Hello, Danny 1992! There are lots of great things to do in my city.
Here are some ideas:

💼 Go to the _____. It costs about _____, and *it takes about / you need about* _____ .

💼 Try to see the _____. I think it costs about _____

💼 Visit the _____. It's *near / next to / on the corner of* _____. It's free!

Enjoy your visit!

REPLY   ◀ PREVIOUS | NEXT ▶

E Read your options to your classmates. Decide which ones make the best use of Danny's time and money.

REFLECT … How can the skill of establishing priorities be useful to you in **Work and Career** and **Study and Learning**?

Language wrap-up

A Look at this map. Complete the place names with words from the box. (4 points)

gallery
station
centre
museum

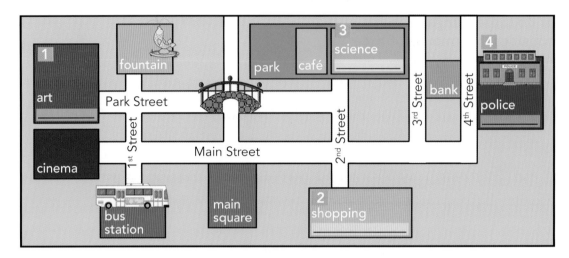

B Look at the map in Exercise A again and complete the sentences. (6 points)

1 You are at the bus station _____ 1ˢᵗ Street. Take the second right, go
_____ the bridge and turn left. Go straight ahead and the _____ is in the
park, _____ the café.

2 You are in the main square. Turn right and go straight ahead. Then take the third left.
The _____ is on the right _____ the bank.

> **8 – 10 correct:** I can talk about places and attractions in a city and ask for and give directions.
>
> **0 – 7 correct:** Look again at the Vocabulary sections on pages 59 and 62.
>
> **SCORE:**   /10

Read the descriptions below. Choose the correct options to complete the text. (10 points)

In Granada, there **(1)** is / are a fantastic Moorish monument – the Alhambra Palace. It has
(2) any / lots of beautiful designs. The food in Granada is excellent and there **(3)** is / are a
lot of good restaurants. But **(4)** you don't / don't eat in restaurants near the Alhambra –
they're very expensive.

Antigua is a beautiful city. There **(5)** is / are several pretty squares where you can have lunch
or just drink coffee. If possible, **(6)** stay / you stay in a hotel in the main square.
(7) Doesn't / Don't travel in taxis in Antigua. It's small, and it's possible to walk everywhere.

Ko Samui is a fantastic island. There aren't **(8)** some / many cars and you can relax
completely. The restaurants and cafes are very friendly and there is **(9)** a lot of / many good
food. Sometimes **(10)** there is / are traditional dances.

> **8 – 10 correct:** I can use *there is*, *there are*, and quantifiers to describe where I live.
> I can use the imperative to give directions and instructions.
>
> **0 – 7 correct:** Look again at the Grammar sections on pages 58 and 61.
>
> **SCORE:**   /10

WRITING WORKSHOP

A Read the two emails and answer the questions below.

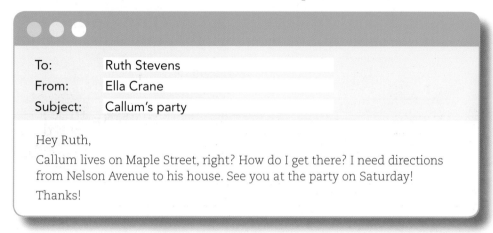

To: Ruth Stevens
From: Ella Crane
Subject: Callum's party

Hey Ruth,
Callum lives on Maple Street, right? How do I get there? I need directions from Nelson Avenue to his house. See you at the party on Saturday!
Thanks!

To: Ella Crane
From: Ruth Stevens
Subject: Callum's party

Hi Ella,
OK, here are the directions. Go down Nelson Avenue to Main Street. Then turn right and go onto the motorway. Go about three miles and take the second exit onto Park Avenue. Take the first left and go under the bridge. Go straight ahead for about two miles then turn right onto Maple Street. Go over the bridge, and then go about 200 yards. Callum's house is number 220, on the left.

Don't worry – call me on my mobile if you get lost! See you there.

1   What is the purpose of the first email? The second email?
2   Is the style of the emails formal or informal? How do you know?
3   In your opinion, are Ruth's directions clear or unclear? Why?

B Look back at the emails and complete sentences 1–3 with the correct words from the text. Choose the correct option to complete sentence 4.

1   The two informal words the friends use for greetings are ——————— and ———————.
2   Ella asks for directions to Callum's house with the question, ———————————————.
3   Ella closes her email with the word ———————.
4   To give directions, Ruth uses the present simple / imperative form of the verbs.

C **Work in pairs. Write an email asking your partner for directions from your school to his/her house.**

D **Exchange emails. Write an email answer giving directions to your house.**

HOW ARE YOU DOING?

Look back at your writing and tick the statements that are true.
◯ The directions are easy to understand.
◯ The phrases for giving directions are correct.
◯ The prepositions of place are correct.
Now ask your partner to look at your writing and tick.
Are the directions clear and easy to understand?

● Well done!   ● Nearly!   ● Think again!

UNIT 6 DIFFERENT STROKES

IN THIS UNIT YOU

- learn language for talking about your life and your lifestyle
- listen for specific numbers in personal profiles
- write sentences about a green lifestyle
- read personal profiles from an online dating site
- talk to an old friend about your life now
- analyse different aspects of your lifestyle and decide what things you want to change
- ▶ watch a video about ways to be green

LISTENING
for numerical information
How many situations can you think of in which you have to listen for and understand numerical information?

WRITING
simple sentences
Look at the writing section in this unit. What two things do all grammatically correct sentences have in English?

LIFE SKILLS

SELF & SOCIETY

making personal change Why do we sometimes want to make changes in our lives? What kinds of changes do people often make?

A Tick (✓) the things on this page that are a big part of your life. Think of other things that are also very important in your life, e.g. pets, other hobbies, etc.

entertainment

shopping

food

exercise

Your Life

social relationships

HOW TO SAY IT

Talking about lifestyles

Food/Shopping is a big part of my life.

My friends / Animals are a big part of my life.

Why do/don't you like …?

Our lifestyles are very/quite different because …

B Work in small groups. Compare the things that are important in your lives. Do most people in your group have very similar or very different lifestyles?

A: *Food is a big part of my life. I like going to restaurants, but I also like cooking at home.*
B: *Me, too. I don't usually go to restaurants, but I often cook at home.*

Different strokes

A Look at these different lifestyles. Write each word from the box under the lifestyle it describes.

relaxing   healthy   boring   stressful   unhealthy   wasteful   green   exciting

1 _____

2 _____

3 _____

4 _____

5 _____

6 _____

7 _____

8 _____

B Look back at the adjectives in Exercise A. How many different endings do you notice? Do all of the adjectives have a special ending?

C Work in pairs. Talk about the type of lifestyle you and your family have. Give reasons.

A: *My mum has a healthy lifestyle. She plays sport and she eats healthy food.*
B: *Really? Well, my dad is 65 now, so his life isn't very …*

A Read the profiles. Where do you think they come from?

a) an online dating agency   b) a website about famous people   c) an online English course

Youandme.com   Home ♥ Account ♥ Login

FIND YOUR PERFECT DATE

Name: Sam
Age: 22
Likes: rock music; animals; fast food; surfing
Dislikes: studying; football; the winter
My lifestyle is: exciting!
Right now: I'm working in a music shop.

Name: Christina
Age: 19
Likes: reading; cooking; animals; going to the ballet
Dislikes: football; loud music; cold weather
My lifestyle is: healthy!
Right now: I am a university student.

B Work in pairs. Answer the questions.

1 What do Christina and Sam have in common?
2 In what ways are they different?
3 In your opinion, is it a good idea for them to go out with each other?

A: *She likes the ballet but he likes rock music.*
B: *Yes, but they both ....*

LISTENING: for numerical information

When you hear a number, think about the way it looks. This helps you understand what it is (e.g. a date, a time, a year, or a phone number). To help you remember a number, say it in your head when you are writing it down.

A Read these figures. Match them to what you think they refer to.

1	034 186 2864		a)	a year
2	30/11/98		b)	a time
3	12.52		c)	a person's age
4	1998		d)	a phone number
5	24		e)	a date

HOW TO SAY IT

0 can be said as both **zero** and **oh**.

B 🔊 31 **Listen and repeat the numbers in Exercise A.**

C 🔊 32 **Listen to the statements. Write the numbers you hear. Practise saying the numbers in English in your head when you are writing them down.**

1 _____ 2 _____ 3 _____ 4 _____ 5 _____

D 🔊 33 **Listen to three profiles from a school reunion website. Complete the information below.**

School Reunion

Tom Edwards

Paul Newton

Vanessa Hughes

NAME: Tom Edwards
SCHOOL GRADUATION YEAR:
(1) _____
DATE OF SCHOOL REUNION:
(2) _____ March

NAME: Paul Newton
DATE OF SCHOOL REUNION:
(3) _____ August
PHONE NUMBER:
(4) _____

NAME: Vanessa Hughes
REUNION FOR YEAR:
(5) _____
SCHOOL REUNION AT:
(6) _____
ON: (7) _____

A 🎧 **34 LANGUAGE IN CONTEXT** Listen to part of a conversation. Do Jonathan and Sophia know each other well? How do you know?

Jonathan: It's nice to meet you in person, Sophia, and not just on the dating website.

Sophia: It's nice to meet you, too.

Jonathan: So ... are you meeting lots of people on the New Friends website?

Sophia: Not really. You're the first, so I'm a little nervous!

Jonathan: Yeah, me too. Well, tell me about yourself. You're studying dentistry, right?

Sophia: Yes, but I'm just studying part time this term. I'm also working as a receptionist at a dental clinic. What about you?

Jonathan: I'm a student, too. I'm studying robotics. Oh, you're not eating your burger. Do you want something different?

Sophia: Oh, no. It's fine! I'm just not very hungry. Um ... are you working, too, or just studying?

Jonathan: I'm just studying, but I want to work during the summer holidays.

NOTICE!

Is the conversation about the people's routine activities or about activities during this period in their lives?

B ANALYSE Read the conversation in Exercise A again.

Form Choose the correct option to complete the sentence below. Then complete the table.

We form the present continuous with ...

a) be + verb + -ing.

b) be + base form of verb.

Affirmative	Negative	Yes/No question	Short answer	Wh- question
I'm working.	I'm not (1) _____.		Yes, I (3) _____. No, I'm not.	
He's/She's/It's working.	He/She/It isn't working.	Is he/she/it working?	Yes, he/she/it is. No, he/she/it isn't.	Where is he/she/it working?
We're/They're working.	We/They aren't working.	(2) _____ you/they working?	Yes, we/they are. No, we/they aren't.	Where (4) _____ you/they working?

Function Choose the correct option to complete the sentence.

The present continuous is used with situations or events that ...

a) happen all the time and are permanent routines.

b) are happening at the moment of speaking or during this period of time in the person's life.

Spelling rules

When the verb ends in -e,	drop the e before adding -ing. e.g. take – tak**ing**, make – mak**ing**, live – liv**ing**
When a one-syllable verb ends in consonant–vowel–consonant,	double the final consonant, then add -ing. e.g. plan – pla**nning**, get – ge**tting**, stop – sto**pping**

C PRACTISE Complete these sentences with the present continuous form of the verbs in brackets.

1 At the moment, I _____ (*make*) a sandwich for lunch.
2 _____ you _____ (*have*) a good time?
3 What _____ you _____ (*do*) these days?
4 Sally _____ (*not talk*) to me at the moment. I don't know why.
5 Come on! We _____ (*wait*) for you!
6 At the moment, Adele _____ (*live*) in Montreal.

D 🔊 **NOW YOU DO IT** Work in small groups. Talk about things that are happening at this time in your life.

At the moment I'm not working, so I'm living with my parents. I'm looking for a new job.

PRONUNCIATION: /ŋ/

A 🔊 **35** Listen to these pairs of words and phrases. Are the sounds of the <u>underlined</u> letters the same or different? Now listen again and repeat the words.

thi<u>n</u>   thi<u>ng</u>   walk-<u>in</u>   walk<u>ing</u>

B 🔊 **36** Listen and practise these words. Pay special attention to your pronunciation of the *-ng* endings.

walking	planning	living	song
working	doing	taking	wrong
thinking	sitting	standing	young

C 🔊 **37** Work in pairs. Practise these conversations. Correct each other's pronunciation of the *-ng* endings when necessary. Listen and check.

1 A: What's Mum doing?
  B: She's talking on the phone.
2 A: Why are you singing?
  B: Because this is my favourite song.
3 A: Where are you working these days?
  B: I'm not working. I'm studying engineering.

SPEAKING: talking to an old friend

A Tick (✓) the questions you could ask an old friend to find out about their life now.

☐ How are you?
☐ Where are you working at the moment?
☐ What are you doing these days?
☐ How old are you?
☐ When is your birthday?
☐ What are you studying?
☐ What's your name?
☐ Are you going out with anyone?
☐ How is your family?
☐ Where are you living now?

B 🔊 Work in pairs. You are old friends who meet in the street. Ask and answer the ticked questions from Exercise A.

A: *Hi! How are you?*
B: *I'm fine! How about you?*
A: *I'm good, thanks. And how is your family?*

A Amy has a very green lifestyle. Match the words and phrases to the pictures. Use the red boxes.

1 save water
2 turn off the lights
3 recycle
4 cycle to university/work

5 buy organic food
6 reuse bags
7 get a lift
8 pick up litter

B Do you have a green lifestyle? Tick (✓) the things from Exercise A that you do to help the environment. Use the blue boxes.

C Work in groups. Ask your classmates questions to find out who has a green lifestyle. Make notes of your classmates' answers.

A: *Do you cycle to work?*
B: *No, I don't, but I get a lift with a colleague. What about you?*

D Share the information with your classmates. Is anyone similar to Amy?

I think Irina has a green lifestyle. She cycles to school every day and she buys organic fruit and vegetables.

GRAMMAR: present continuous vs present simple

A LANGUAGE IN CONTEXT Read this extract from a newsletter. What does Adam want his parents to do?

ACT GREEN NEWSLETTER

This month we're asking our readers to help their friends and family to 'act green'. Here is what one reader says:

My parents don't have a very green lifestyle! They live in Arizona, and they use a lot of electricity for air conditioning. My dad always forgets to turn off his computer at night, and that uses a lot of electricity, too. They also water their garden a lot. But they know the environment is important, and they're trying to change some things.

Now they're turning off the air conditioning and opening windows in the mornings when it's cool. They're turning off lights and computers when they're not using them. I'm helping them plant cactus and other plants that don't need much water in their garden, so they're using less water now.

Adam Hunter

> **NOTICE!**
>
> Look back at the text. Circle the verbs in green that are in the present simple and underline the verbs that are in the present continuous.

B ANALYSE Read the text in Exercise A again.

Function Match 1–2 to a–b to complete the sentences.
1 The verbs in the present simple describe   a) things happening right now or around now.
2 The verbs in the present continuous describe   b) things that are generally true or permanent situations.

We don't use the present continuous with some verbs:
e.g. *like, know, want, need*.

C PRACTISE Choose the correct options to complete the sentences.
1 What are you doing / do you do at the moment?
2 Pete is listening / listens to his MP3 player at the moment.
3 I usually have / am having lunch at around 1pm.
4 My cousin wants / is wanting to be a DJ when he leaves school.
5 This food is delicious. I am liking / like it!
6 At the moment, Mum is having / has Spanish lessons.

D NOW YOU DO IT Write four sentences about your life in general and four sentences about your life at the moment. One of your sentences should be false. Read them to the class for them to guess which one is false.

WRITING: simple sentences

Simple statements in English always have a subject and a verb, and often have an object, e.g.
I   like   cats and dogs.
Subject + verb + object
They usually appear in this order: subject – verb – object.

A Double-underline the subjects of the sentences below and write S.
Circle the verbs and write V. Underline the objects and write O.

  S   V   O
I (re-use) plastic bags.

1 People waste a lot of water.

2 Ian is reading an article about recycling.

3 We recycle all our paper.

B Write one sentence about each situation. Make sure you include a subject, verb and object in the correct order.

1 _____   2 _____   3 _____

C Work in pairs. Compare your sentences. Correct any mistakes.

LifeSkills

MAKING PERSONAL CHANGE

- Understand what you are doing and not doing right in different areas of your life.
- Decide what you want to change.
- Make an action plan; consider what changes are realistic and how much time you need to make each change.

A Look at the lifestyle table and the example. For each category, write things you are doing right and things you are doing wrong at this point in your life. Then circle the number that best indicates where you are in each category.

Lifestyle category	Things I'm doing right	Things I'm doing wrong	My score Wrong OK Right
Being green	I'm using canvas shopping bags now, not plastic.	I'm not recycling. I'm using a lot of electricity and water. I never use public transport.	1 ②3 4 5

Lifestyle category	Things I'm doing right	Things I'm doing wrong	My score Wrong OK Right
Being green			1 2 3 4 5
Healthy living			1 2 3 4 5
Work or study			1 2 3 4 5
Social relationships			1 2 3 4 5

B Tick (✓) one category in the table in Exercise A that you want to change. Here are some ideas for how to decide on a category.

- An area with many problems: making big changes is very exciting!
- An area with not many problems: sometimes it's better to start with small changes!
- An area that you are worrying about: it's good to make changes that are important to you!

C Make a realistic action plan similar to this one.

AREA I WANT TO MAKE CHANGES IN:

Social relationships

General changes to make	Specific plans	Time
Spend more time with my family	1 Cook dinner for my parents 2 Babysit my brother's children	1 Next Saturday 2 One night every month
Have more fun	1 Go out with my best friend 2 Have a party at my house 3 Join a club to meet new friends	1 Once a week 2 In the next two months 3 In the next six months

D Work in pairs. Share your action plan with your partner. Explain what you are planning to do and when you are planning to do it. If you want to, ask questions about your partner's plan.

A: *I'm not having much fun these days so I want to have a party at my house next Saturday.*

B: *That sounds like a great idea!*

HOW TO SAY IT

Talking about plans
I want to / need to …, so I'm planning to …
I'm planning to …
What are you planning to do …?

REFLECT … How can the skill of making personal change be useful to you in **Work and Career** and **Study and Learning**?

Language wrap-up

A Read what people say about their lifestyles. Write the opposite of the adjective in **bold** to complete the sentences. (4 points)

1 My lifestyle is quite **healthy**. I exercise a lot and eat fruit. My boyfriend watches TV or plays video games all day. He has a very _____ lifestyle.

2 I work in an office every day. I guess my lifestyle is **boring**. My brother has a really _____ lifestyle. He's a police officer.

3 My sister has a really **relaxing** lifestyle. She studies in the morning and goes to the gym in the afternoon. Her husband has a very _____ life. He works from 8am to 9pm every day, including Saturdays.

4 I try to be **green**. I recycle everything. My parents are really _____, though. They throw everything away and they never recycle.

B Jerry is talking about his green lifestyle. Complete these sentences with words from the box. (6 points)

organic   lights   reuse   save   cycle   get

'I try to have a green lifestyle. I (1) _____ water and I always turn off the (2) _____ before I go to bed. My office is pretty close to my flat, so I usually (3) _____ to work. Sometimes I (4) _____ a lift with a friend to go to the supermarket. I always buy (5) _____ fruit and vegetables and I always (6) _____ bags.'

---

8 – 10 correct: I can talk about different lifestyles.

0 – 7 correct: Look again at the Vocabulary sections on pages 70 and 74.

SCORE: /10

Read more of what Jerry says. Complete the text with the verbs in brackets in the present simple or present continuous. (10 points)

'I (1) _____ (not know) why people are so wasteful. At the moment, I (2) _____ (read) a great book about protecting the planet. Everyone (3) _____ (know) that traffic is a problem. It's obvious that people (4) _____ (destroy) the planet. Some people (5) _____ (need) to use a car sometimes, but not every day. Walk or cycle! I usually (6) _____ (work) in the city centre and I always (7) _____ (cycle) to work. At the moment though, I (8) _____ (work) from home, so I don't need to travel anywhere! I know people (9) _____ (not agree) with everything I say, but now I think people (10) _____ (learn) that they need to do more to protect the planet.'

---

8 – 10 correct: I can contrast the present simple and the present continuous to talk about general time and what is happening now or around now.

0 – 7 correct: Look again at the Grammar sections on pages 72 and 74.

SCORE: /10

A Read the conversation. Complete the conversation with the sentences in the box.

> What about you?   How are you?   I'm an accountant.   And do you have a family?
> It's great to see you!   So, what are you doing these days?

James: Molly? Molly Evans?

Molly: Oh my gosh! James Burton! Wow! (1) _____

James: I'm fine. (2) _____
Do you live near here?

Molly: Nice to see you, too. Yes, I live just a few streets from here. (3) _____

James: No, I live in the Cedar Hills area, but I'm visiting friends over here.

Molly: (4) _____

James: Well, I'm working at Tracon Industries. I'm an industrial engineer.

Molly: Oh, that's great! I work at an architecture firm, but I'm not an architect.
(5) _____

James: (6) _____

Molly: No, I'm not married.

James: I'm single, too. Hey, um, are you seeing anyone? I mean, can I call you some time?

Molly: Well, uh, OK. Why not? My mobile number is 415 836 7521.

James: Got it! OK, talk to you soon!

Molly: Sure! Great to see you!

B Find and <u>underline</u> the following things in the conversation in Exercise A.

* Two expressions of surprise
* A positive reaction
* A general question about the other person's life
* Three specific questions about the other person's life

C Work in pairs. Imagine that you and your partner are old friends and that you are meeting after several years. Roleplay a conversation about your lives now.

Things to include:
* greetings
* at least two expressions of surprise
* at least one general question
* at least three specific questions
* an ending to the conversation

D Now work with a different partner. Have a similar conversation with that person. Try to remember to include things from the list in Exercise C.

HOW ARE YOU DOING?

Think about your speaking. Do you feel confident using:
○ greetings and endings to conversations?
○ questions about people's lives?
○ expressions of surprise?
How do you feel about your speaking generally?

● ○ ●
Very confident   Not sure …   Need to practise

UNIT 7 YOU'VE GOT TALENT!

IN THIS UNIT YOU

- learn language for talking about personalities and abilities
- read a text about personalities according to theories of astrology
- use phrases to show interest in a conversation
- write a reference describing someone's personality
- listen to a review of a TV talent show describing someone's abilities
- plan an event based on people's abilities
- ▶ watch a video about people with different abilities

SPEAKING
showing interest

In what ways can people show interest in a conversation? How do you feel when someone does not show interest in what you are saying?

READING
for the main idea

How can you quickly know what a text is about?

LIFE SKILLS

WORK & CAREER

working as a group to do a task In what situations do you have to work with other people in a group? When you work in a group, do you prefer to be a leader or a follower? Why?

A Look at these photos. In your opinion, who is the most talented? Why?

HOW TO SAY IT

Talking about yourself

I play the guitar / speak French / run marathons.
I play the guitar / dance / cook very well.
I'm a good guitar player / runner / football player.
I'm good at playing the guitar / dancing / cooking.

B Are you talented? Tell your classmates what talents you have. Use the ideas below and your own ideas.

play the guitar   speak French   dance   cook   play football

A: Let's see … I play the guitar. I speak Italian and French.
B: I think I'm talented. I'm a good football player, and I also play basketball.
C: I'm good at cooking and I'm a good dancer, too.

A Match the personality adjectives to the statements.

1	friendly	a)	I'm happy. I think my life is great.
2	generous	b)	I'm good at making plans.
3	patient	c)	I usually do very well in my exams.
4	reliable	d)	I love buying things for other people.
5	optimistic	e)	I never tell lies.
6	organised	f)	I make friends easily.
7	clever	g)	My friends can depend on me.
8	honest	h)	I'm good at waiting for things.

B Work in pairs. Look at the photos. Say what adjectives from Exercise A you think describe these people.

Bill Gates

David Beckham

Angelina Jolie

I think Bill Gates is really clever because …

C Work in pairs. Tell your partner which positive qualities from Exercise A you think you have and why.

I think I'm optimistic. I'm usually happy.

A 38 Listen to the conversation. Then choose T (true) or F (false) for each statement.

1	Jenny is applying for a job.	T / F
2	Jonathan thinks Carmen has good qualities for an English teacher.	T / F
3	Carmen probably makes friends easily.	T / F
4	She isn't good at planning.	T / F
5	Carmen speaks Spanish.	T / F
6	She is patient when people are learning something.	T / F

B Read Jenny's reference. Then think about your best friend and his/her ideal job. Write a personal reference for your friend.

To whom it may concern,

I'm writing this reference for my friend Carmen Dean. In my opinion, she is ideal for a job as an English teacher for several reasons.

Firstly, Carmen is a very friendly person. She likes meeting new people, and she loves talking to people. Secondly, Carmen is very organised and reliable. She's good at making plans, and people can depend on her. Finally, she is very patient. She is helping a friend with his Spanish, and she often explains things several times.

I definitely recommend Carmen Dean for a job as an English teacher.

Yours faithfully,

Jenny Richards

READING: for the main idea page 60 ⚙

When you read for the main idea, look quickly at the text to find key words or phrases. These can tell you the subject of each paragraph. Key words are often nouns or adjectives.

A Look quickly at paragraph 1 in the text below. Circle the nouns and underline the adjectives. Based on these words, what do you think the text is about?

B Now look quickly at paragraphs 2–4. Circle the nouns and underline the adjectives.

C Look at the key words you identified in all four paragraphs and write these headings in the correct places in the text.

Health   Good qualities   Bad luck!   Work and money

D Read the paragraphs more carefully. Check your answers to Exercise C.

MYSTIC MIKE SAYS: 🐟

1 _____
First of all, people born on 29th February are unlucky! They only have one birthday every four years! But because of this, they have special talents and abilities.

2 _____
They are very friendly and optimistic. They always see the positive side of life. They are fun, and many of them can sing or dance very well. They've got lots of friends and they are always loyal to them.

3 _____
People born on 29th February like their jobs and they want to be rich. But they don't usually give presents because they aren't very generous!

4 _____
These Pisceans usually have a healthy lifestyle. They eat lots of fruit and vegetables and they are good at sport.

E 🎧 Work in groups. Answer these questions.

1 Was anyone you know born on 29th February? Do you agree with the text? Why or why not?

2 Do you read your horoscope? Do you think astrology influences a person's personality?

GRAMMAR: can/can't – ability

A LANGUAGE IN CONTEXT Match the photos to people's statements about their pets.

CAN YOUR PET PLAY A SPORT? OR SING? OR DANCE?

Post comments about your pet's unusual talents!
The most talented pet will win a prize of £500!

Yes, he can. **My horse can play football!** He's really talented!

J.T. Williams, Texas

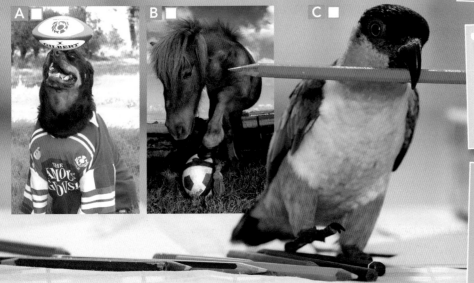

A ☐   B ☐   C ☐

My parrot can't talk, but he can draw. He draws pictures with coloured pencils!

Nina, Brazil

Our dog, Muffin, can balance things on his nose. It's very funny!

Mrs Hill, Scotland

B ANALYSE Read the texts in Exercise A again.

Form Choose the correct option to complete the sentences. Then complete the examples in the table.

1 After *can* we use _____ .   a) a verb   b) a noun
2 The contraction of *cannot* is _____ .   a) *can't*   b) *cant*
3 The correct form after *he/she/it* is _____ .   a) *can*   b) *cans*

NOTICE!
What word do the people use to talk about abilities?

Affirmative	Negative	Questions	Short answers
It can fly.	He can't play football.	Can they swim?	Yes, he can. / No, he can't.
You (1) _____ sing! We (2) _____ speak English.	I (3) _____ cook Japanese food. Jamal and Pierre (4) _____ speak Chinese.	(5) _____ you play the guitar? (6) _____ you and Carla drive?	No, I (7) _____ . Yes, we (8) _____ .

Function Choose the correct option to complete the sentences.

1 We use *can/can't* to talk about _____ .
   a) routine activities   b) abilities
2 We use *can/can't* to refer to _____ .
   a) people   b) animals   c) people and animals

WHAT'S RIGHT?
◯ She can to dance.
◯ She can dance.
◯ She cans dance.

C PRACTISE Complete these sentences with *can* or *can't* and the correct form of the verb in brackets.

1 A: *Can* they *play* (play) tennis?   B: Yes, they _____ .
2 Sally is a great chef. She _____ (cook) French food.
3 I _____ (not open) the door. Can you?
4 A: _____ Angela _____ (speak) Japanese?   B: No, she _____ .
5 A: _____ he _____ (play) the guitar?   B: Yes, he _____ .
6 We _____ (not hear) the TV. Please turn down your music.

D 🗣 **NOW YOU DO IT** Work in pairs. Ask and answer questions about each other's abilities. Use the phrases below.

- cook Italian food
- swim five kilometres
- sing opera
- dance salsa
- play badminton

A: *Can you swim five kilometres?*
B: *No, I can't. Can you?*

PRONUNCIATION: *can/can't*

A 🎧 **39** Listen to the pronunciation of *can* and *can't* in these sentences. Which form is stronger and which is weaker? Mark them S (strong) or W (weak). Then choose the correct option to complete the sentences below.

1   I can ☐ speak French, but I can't ☐ cook French food.
2   I can ☐ play the violin.
3   I can't ☐ sing and I can't ☐ dance!
4   I can't ☐ drive a car, but I can ☐ ride a bike.

a)   When we use *can* alone or before *can't*, the pronunciation is strong / weak.
b)   When we use *can* after *can't*, the pronunciation is strong / weak.
c)   The pronunciation of *can't* is always strong / weak.

B 🗣 🎧 **40** Practise the sentences below. Then listen, check and repeat.

1   My sister can dance, but she can't sing.
2   I can't speak German, but I can understand some words.
3   I can't ride a motorbike, but I can drive a car.
4   I can hear you, but I can't see you!

VOCABULARY: talents and abilities

A Complete these sentences with phrases from the box.

can sing   can play   am good at   can speak   can cook   can drive

1   I _____ the guitar.
2   I _____ karate.
3   I _____ a car.
4   I _____ a foreign language.
5   I _____ opera.
6   I _____ French food.

B 🗣 Work in groups. Which statements in Exercise A are true for you? What other things can you do? Use ideas from the box as well as your own ideas.

salsa dancing   a lorry   traditional songs   surfing   healthy snacks
Italian   karaoke songs   many languages

A: *I can play the guitar. What about you?*
B: *I can't play the guitar but I can play the piano.*
C: *I can't play the guitar or the piano but I can cook French food.*

C 🗣 Tell the class about a talented person in your group.

We think Emanuel is talented because he is good at salsa dancing, he can play chess, and …

A Look at this picture. What kind of TV show is it? Do you have TV shows like this in your country?

B 🔊 **41** Listen to a man giving his opinion on the TV talent show *Dream Stars*. Choose the correct option to complete the sentences.

1 Some of the dancers / singers on *Dream Stars* are not very talented.
2 The man thinks the dancers can / can't dance very well.
3 *Can You Dance?* is a British / an American show.
4 The woman says that most comedians can / can't make her laugh.
5 The man thinks most of the comedians on *Dream Stars* are / are not very funny.
6 In general, the man likes / doesn't like the show.

C 🗣 Work in pairs. Discuss these questions.

1 Which TV talent shows do you like? Why?
2 Which TV talent shows don't you like? Why not?

A: *I like* The X Factor *because it's interesting.*
B: *Really? I don't like it. The contestants can't sing!*

GRAMMAR: adverbs of manner

A LANGUAGE IN CONTEXT Read what a judge on a talent show thinks about one of the contestants. Is the judge's general impression of Ryan positive or negative?

Contestant	Genre	Notes
Ryan Gleason Age: 24 Nationality: Irish	comedian	Ryan is very clever and talented. He tells great jokes, but he isn't very organised. That's why he sometimes can't remember his jokes very well. He also speaks very **quickly** and very **quietly**. But Ryan is a very funny guy, and I think we can help him learn to speak **slowly** and **clearly**. He learns fast, and his audience loves him.

NOTICE!
Look back at the words in **bold**. How are they similar?

B ANALYSE Read the notes in Exercise A again.

Function Choose the correct option to complete the sentence.
Adverbs of manner describe things or people / actions.

Form Choose the correct option to complete the sentences. Then complete the table with the adverb forms of the adjectives.

1 We form adverbs from adjectives. Adverbs usually end in -ity / -ly.
2 Adverbs of manner usually come before / after the verb.

Most adjectives: add -ly		Adjectives ending in -y: change y to i and add -ly	Irregular adverbs
wonderful – wonderfully	quiet – _____	happy – happily	good – well
slow – slowly	nice – _____	funny – funnily	fast – fast
clear – clearly	bad – _____	noisy – _____	
quick – quickly		angry – _____	

WHAT'S RIGHT?
○ She can speak English well.
○ She can speak well English.
○ She speaks English good.
○ She speaks good English.

C PRACTISE Rewrite these sentences using the verb in brackets and an appropriate adverb of manner.

1   Helen is good at French.
    Helen *can speak French well*. (*speak French*)
2   Our teacher always gives clear explanations.
    Our teacher _____ . (*explain things*)
3   Paul isn't a fast runner.
    Paul can't _____ . (*run*)
4   Tom and Ellie are loud talkers.
    Tom and Ellie _____ . (*talk*)
5   You are a quick learner.
    You _____ . (*learn*)
6   I'm not a good swimmer.
    I can't _____ (*swim*)

D **NOW YOU DO IT** Work in groups. Tell your group about at least two things you do well and two things you don't do well. Use verbs and adverbs from the boxes or your own ideas.

drive   run   sing   talk   speak   cook   dance   draw   paint

quickly   loudly   well   badly   fast   beautifully   slowly   carefully

I can speak English well, and I drive carefully, but I sing badly, and I can't dance very well.

SPEAKING: showing interest

You can show interest in different ways. One way is by using words such as *Wow!* and *Really?* The other is by using your face and your body.

A Look at photos 1 and 2. In which photo does the woman look interested?

B   **42** Listen to the conversations below. <u>Underline</u> the expressions that the people use to show they are interested.

1   A: So, what do you do?
    B: I'm a pilot.
    A: Really? That's amazing! Me, too!

2   A: Do you speak any other languages?
    B: I can speak Chinese.
    A: Wow! Really?

3   A: Can you cook Chinese food?
    B: No, I can't, but I can cook Indian food really well.
    A: Oh, how interesting!

C **43** Listen to the expressions from Exercise B. Practise saying the expressions in an interested way.

D Work in pairs. Talk about things that your family members can do. Remember to use words to show interest.

A: *My sister is good at languages. She can speak Japanese, English, and Portuguese.*
B: *Wow, that's amazing!*

LifeSkills

WORKING AS A GROUP TO DO A TASK

- Break up the big task into smaller tasks and make a list.
- Identify what the group can do together and what each person can do individually.
- Negotiate who can do any remaining tasks. Be flexible!

A 🗣 Work in groups. Your company wants to offer a seminar for small business owners. Read the email from the marketing director. Then decide on at least two more things to do for each category and add them to the list in the attachment.

To:	marketing department (all)
From:	Donald Sanders
Subject:	small business seminar

Hi, all.

We want to offer a seminar for small business owners in this area. The basic ideas are in the attachment. Please work out the details and decide who can do each thing. Can we meet a week from today to discuss?

Thanks.

Project: seminar on business management techniques
Proposed date: Saturday, 1st March
Target audience: local small business owners and managers
Registration fee: £125 per person
Maximum number of participants: 100
Seminar includes: Welcome and introduction to seminar (Lynn Barton, CEO)
Four sessions of 1½ hours each
Lunch
Two coffee breaks
Session topics:
1 Writing or revising your business plan (Steve Ellroy, Business Director)
2 Advertising and promotion: trends and methods (Donald Sanders, Marketing Director)
3 Financial management (Debra Leary, Finance Director)
4 Managing your company's growth (Ben Collins, Market Development Director)

Plan for small business seminar

Things to do			Who does it?
Location	**Promotion**	**Logistics**	
1 Think of several possible locations.	5 Design ad for our website.	9 Make list of equipment (projectors, etc.)	_____
2 Visit locations.	6 Decide on other types of promotion:	10 Order chairs, tables, etc.	_____
3 _____			_____
4 _____	7 _____	11 _____	_____
	8 _____	12 _____	_____
			_____
			_____
			_____

B 🗣 Decide which tasks on the list the whole group can do together. Write G (group) in the *Who does it?* column and the number of those things.

88

C Think about your preferences and abilities. Tick (✓) the appropriate boxes on the survey.

Work with your abilities!

I prefer to work ...
- ⬤ alone.
- ⬤ with other people.

I'm good at ...
- ⬤ drawing or painting.
- ⬤ design.
- ⬤ writing.
- ⬤ talking to people.
- ⬤ organising schedules.
- ⬤ managing people.
- ⬤ managing money.
- ⬤ solving problems.

Submit ➡

D With your group, decide who can do each of the remaining tasks on your list.

A: *I'm good at design, so I can design the ads.*
B: *And I'm good at writing, so maybe I can write the slogans.*
A: *OK, let's do the ads together, then.*
C: *OK, so you and Lisa can do the ads. What about the schedule?*

HOW TO SAY IT

I'm good at ..., so I can ...
I can ... but I can't ...
Can you ...? / What can you do?
Maybe we / you and Gina can ...
because we/you can both ...

? **REFLECT ...** How can the skill of working as a group be useful to you in **Self and Society** and **Study and Learning**?

Language wrap-up

1 VOCABULARY

Complete the text with words from the box. (10 points)

> patient   play   cook   honest   drive   sing   speak   generous   optimistic   clever

My mum is 52. She is very **(1)** _____ and she buys a lot of presents for me and my
brother. She is really good in the kitchen. She can **(2)** _____ delicious food. She is
very **(3)** _____ and never gets angry with my brother or me. She loves to go out with
her friends and **(4)** _____ karaoke. My dad is 54. He is really good at maths and he
can **(5)** _____ Italian and German, so I think he is very **(6)** _____. He can
(7) _____ the piano and the violin, too. My brother, Bruno, really enjoys life and
doesn't worry about the future, so I guess he is very **(8)** _____. He is
(9) _____, too. He doesn't tell lies, and I know I can trust him. He is only 17,
but he can **(10)** _____ a car.

> **8 – 10 correct:** I can talk about people's positive qualities and their abilities.
> **0 – 7 correct:** Look again at the Vocabulary sections on pages 82 and 85.
> **SCORE:**   /10

2 GRAMMAR

A   Write the words in the correct order to form sentences. (6 points)

1   **A:** Francesca / dance / can / well / ? _____

    B: can't / dance / no, / she / well / . _____

2   **A:** sing / can / your sister / ? _____

    B: she / badly / sings / very / no, / . _____

3   **A:** you / swim / can / fast / ? _____

    B: no, / fast / I / swim / can't / . _____

**B   Read the text and find four errors in the use of *can/can't* and adverbs of manner.
Cross them out and correct them. (4 points)**

My cat is a great pet. She can run very fastly and she comes quick when I call her name.
At night, she sleeps quietly in her bed, but in the morning, she miaows loudly for her
breakfast. She cans speak cat language very good!

> **8 – 10 correct:** I can use *can*, *can't*, and adverbs of manner to talk about people's abilities.
> **0 – 7 correct:** Look again at the Grammar sections on pages 84 and 86.
> **SCORE:**   /10

A Read the reference. What four adjectives does Melissa use to describe Bob?

To: Carl Parks
From: Melissa Caldwell
Subject: Reference for Bob Griffin

1 Dear Mr Parks,

2 I'm happy to write a reference for Bob Griffin. 3 I think he is ideal for a job as a sales manager for several reasons.

First, Bob is very reliable. Both friends and colleagues know that they can depend on him. Bob is 4 also friendly and optimistic, and I think this is an important quality for a manager. Finally, 5 Bob is very clever. 6 He learns very quickly.

7 I can definitely recommend Bob Griffin for the job.

8 Yours sincerely,
Melissa Caldwell

B Read the reference again. Then match the parts of the letter to their functions.

a) the reason you are writing _____
b) an introduction to the reasons for the recommendation _____
c) a word to indicate you are adding information _____
d) the closing word or phrase _____
e) a statement about a personal quality _____
f) a final summary sentence _____
g) the greeting _____
h) a reason for your opinion _____

C Choose a partner that you know well and write a personal recommendation for them.

Think about:
• the job they are good for,
• their positive qualities,
• reasons to support your opinion.

Address your recommendation to Ms Karen Jamison.

HOW ARE YOU DOING?

Look back at your writing and tick the statements that are true.
My letter has:
○ a correct greeting and closing.
○ a short opening paragraph with the reason for the letter.
○ at least two opinions about my partner's positive qualities.
○ reasons for these opinions.
○ a final summary sentence.
Now ask your partner to look at your writing and tick.
Is the information clear? Does the writer explain their opinions?

● Well done!   ● Nearly!   ● Think again!

UNIT 8 SHOPPING AROUND

IN THIS UNIT YOU

- learn language for shopping and comparing products
- practise listening to prices in different currencies
- write compound sentences describing products
- learn how to ask shop assistants for help
- read and complete a survey about your shopping habits
- learn a technique for making good choices when deciding what to buy
- ▶ watch a video about shopping

LISTENING
for numerical information

What world currencies can you name in English? Is it difficult for you to understand prices in English? Why or why not?

WRITING
compound sentences

What words do you know in English to connect two sentences? What examples can you find in this unit?

LIFE SKILLS

WORK & CAREER

making choices What kinds of choices do people have to make in their jobs? How do you think you can make good choices?

A Look at these items. Tick (✓) the things that you like to buy.

electronic equipment ☐

food ☐

clothes ☐

accessories ☐

furniture ☐

games ☐

HOW TO SAY IT

Talking about likes and dislikes

I like/love to buy … (but …)

I like/love buying … (but …)

I don't like to shop / shopping for … (but…)

I hate to shop / shopping for … (but…)

B Work in pairs. Talk about the different things you like and don't like to buy. Include things on this page and other things.

A: *I don't like buying furniture but I love shopping for clothes and accessories. What about you?*

B: *I like shopping for food!*

A Match the clothes in the picture to the words.

☐ a jumper
☐ a jacket
☐ trousers
☐ trainers
☐ a dress
☐ a suit
☐ a skirt
☐ a T-shirt
☐ jeans
☐ a shirt
☐ a handbag
☐ a tie
☐ boots
☐ shoes
☐ shorts

B In pairs, talk about clothes you usually/sometimes/never wear.

A: *I usually wear jeans and a T-shirt.*
B: *Me, too. I never wear a suit.*

GRAMMAR: *this, that, these, those*

A **44** **LANGUAGE IN CONTEXT** Listen to the conversation below and look at the picture. What does Sasha decide to wear?

Sasha: I don't know what to wear to the party!
Jenny: How about **that** blue dress?
Sasha: I don't like that one, but I like **this** pink one.
Jenny: Yes, it's nice. OK, and what about **these** shoes?
Sasha: No, those are really old!
Jenny: Well, what about **those** ones over there?
Sasha: The black ones? Yeah, those are fine. Now what about you?
Jenny: Oh, I think these jeans and that purple T-shirt are OK.
Sasha: What about these shoes? They go with jeans.
Jenny: Yes, I really like those ones.

B ANALYSE Read the conversation in Exercise A again.

Form **Choose the correct option to complete the sentences.**

1 We use *this/that* with _____
   a) plural nouns.   b) singular nouns.
2 We use *these/those* with _____
   a) plural nouns.   b) singular nouns.

NOTICE!

Look at the words in **bold** in the conversation. Do they refer to specific things or something in general?

Function **Choose the correct option to complete the sentences.**

1 We use _____ to talk about things that are close to us.
   a) *this/these*   b) *that/those*

2 We use _____ to talk about things that are not very close to us.
   a) *this/these*   b) *that/those*

> It isn't necessary to repeat a noun in the same sentence:
> **Singular:** *I don't like this/that* **T-shirt**, *but I like that/this* **one**.
> **Plural:** *I don't like these/those* **shoes**, *but I like those/these* **ones**.

C PRACTISE Look at the pictures. Complete the sentences with *this*, *that*, *these* or *those*.

1 I really love _____ dress. I wear it all the time.

2 I'd like to wear _____ shorts to the beach today.

3 _____ is my favourite jacket.

4 I can't wear _____ shoes to the party. They're dirty.

D 🎧 NOW YOU DO IT Work in pairs. Look through your book to find pictures of people. Ask and answer questions about the clothes they are wearing.

A: *Do you like those trainers?*
B: *Yes, I do.*
A: *Do you like this T-shirt?*
B: *No, but I like that one.*

WHAT'S RIGHT?
◯ I like this trousers.
◯ I like these trousers.

SPEAKING: asking to try on clothes

A 🔊 45 Listen and number the sentences in the correct order 1–10.

a) Would you like to try on anything else?   ☐
b) OK, I'll take it.   ☐
c) No, it's too small. Do you have it in a size 10?   ☐
d) No, thank you. Here's my credit card.   ☐
e) Can I help you?   [1]
f) Thanks. How much is it?   ☐
g) Yes, here's a 10.   ☐
h) It's fifty pounds.   ☐
i) Yes, please. I'd like to try on this jacket.   ☐
j) Sure. Is that one the right size?   ☐

B Make a list of clothes you need or want to buy in your notebook.

C 🎧 Work in pairs. Student A, you are the assistant. Student B, you are the customer. Ask and answer questions about the clothes on your list in Exercise B. Then switch roles.

A: *Can I help you?*
B: *Yes, I'd like to try on these jeans.*
A: *Of course. Are those the right size?*

When you are listening to the price of something, try to write down the numbers as you hear them. You can then check the price by repeating it.

A 🎧 **46** Write each unit of currency under the correct price tag. Then listen and repeat.

yen	cents	dollars	pounds	euros	pence

$1,500	¥385	10p	€127,395	£12,400	50¢
1	2	3	4	5	6

> **HOW TO SAY IT** 🗣
>
> *75p = seventy-five pence / seventy-five 'p'*

B 🎧 **47** Listen to the conversations. Match each conversation to the correct price.

Conversation 1: ☐   Conversation 2: ☐   Conversation 3: ☐   Conversation 4: ☐

a) €235,450   b) £17.68   c) $560   d) ¥999

C 🎧 **48** Listen to the ads for these items. Write how much they cost.

1 _____   2 _____   3 _____   4 _____

D 🗣 Work in pairs. Discuss how much each item in Exercise C costs in your own currency. Guess how much they cost in other countries.

> **HOW TO SAY IT** 🗣
>
> *I think it costs about …*
> *I don't think so.*
> *OK, let's say it costs …*

A Match the adjectives to the correct definitions.

When a gadget is …

1	attractive		a)	it is easy to use.
2	up-to-date		b)	it doesn't cost a lot of money.
3	user-friendly		c)	it is small.
4	compact		d)	it costs a lot of money.
5	versatile		e)	it can do lots of different things.
6	expensive		f)	it is strong and works well.
7	powerful		g)	it looks good.
8	cheap		h)	it is very modern.

B Read the conversation below. Complete the sentences with words from Exercise A.

A: Can you tell me about this mobile phone?

B: Yes, sure. I love this mobile because it's so easy to use – it really is (1) _____. And it's also very (2) _____. You can listen to music, go online and it has a digital camera, too.

A: Yeah, that's great. Is it (3) _____?

B: No, it's actually very cheap …

C 🗣 Work in pairs. Student A is an assistant in an electronics shop. Student B is a customer. Ask and answer questions about the items below. Then switch roles.

> MP3 player   memory stick   digital camera
> mobile phone   laptop

A: *Can you tell me about this laptop?*

B: *Yes, sure. It's versatile. It can do lots of different things.*

A Read the survey about Ramón's shopping habits. Answer the questions.

Consumer survey

Please take about 5 minutes to complete our questionnaire! All information is confidential.

Age: 23   Male ✓   Female ◯   Country: UK

Type of item	How often do you buy it?	Where do you usually buy it?	How do you usually pay for it?	About how much do you spend on it per year?
clothes, shoes & accessories	twice a month	shops	credit card	£600
books/magazines/e-books	once a month	shops	cash	£240
music (CDs or downloads)	every week	online	debit card	£780
films (DVDs, downloads, rentals)	three times a month	online	debit card	£150
computers & accessories	once every three years	shops	cheque	£320
phones & accessories	once or twice a year	shops	credit card	£60
other electronics & accessories (tablets, e-readers, game equipment)	never			

Thank you for completing our questionnaire!

1 Where does Ramón usually buy CDs?
2 How much does he spend on films per year?
3 How does he usually pay for books and magazines?
4 What does he buy only once or twice a year?
5 What does he pay for by credit card?

B Now read this conversation. Ramón is talking about his survey results with his friend Jay. Who spends more money on clothes?

Jay: Do you buy a lot of books?

Ramón: I guess so. I buy about two books every month. I always buy e-books online, and I pay by debit card.

Jay: What about clothes? How much do you spend on clothes per year?

Ramón: Well, I spend about £50 a month, so about £600 a year. What about you?

Jay: I don't spend any money on clothes. I spend about £800 a year on films!

C Work in pairs. Copy the survey above and complete it for yourself. Then discuss your shopping habits with your partner. Use the conversation in Exercise B to help you.

HOW TO SAY IT

Talking about shopping habits
I usually pay (in) cash.
*   by (debit/credit) card.*
*   by cheque.*

A 🎧 **49** Listen to the conversations. <u>Underline</u> the words that the speaker stresses in his answers to clarify the correct information.

1 A: Is this my mobile?
   B: No, this is mine. That one is yours.

2 A: Are these my bags?
   B: No, those are your bags. These are mine.

B 🗣 Work in pairs. <u>Underline</u> the stressed words in the answers.

1 A: Do you like that sofa?
   B: No, I don't like that one, but I like this one.

2 A: Is this David's book?
   B: No, this is mine. That one over there is David's book.

3 A: Do you have this CD?
   B: No, I don't have that one, but I have this one.

C 🗣 🎧 **50** Practise the conversations in Exercise B. Then listen and check.

GRAMMAR: comparative adjectives

A LANGUAGE IN CONTEXT Read this review. Then choose the correct option to complete the statement.

ARE YOU LOOKING FOR THE PERFECT FATHER'S DAY GIFT?

Then how about the new Reader Plus e-reader? With this e-reader, Dad can download all his favourite books and magazines, but that's not all! The Reader Plus also has a camera! It's a little more expensive than other e-readers, but it's less expensive than a tablet. It's **bigger** than other e-readers, but **smaller** than most tablets, so it's better than a tablet for reading in bed. Also, other e-readers are a lot **heavier** than the Reader Plus. The Reader Plus is more versatile than other e-readers and **easier** to use than a tablet. I'm giving the Reader Plus 4.5 stars!

★★★★⯪

Review by Ian Hodge, Bedford

NOTICE!

Look at the forms of the adjectives in red. What is the base form of each adjective?

The writer _____.

a) talks about the Reader Plus

b) compares the Reader Plus with other e-readers

B ANALYSE Read the review in Exercise A again.

Function Choose the correct option to complete the sentence.
We use comparative forms to compare two things / more than two things.

WHAT'S RIGHT?

◯ He's less old.
◯ He's younger.

Form Write the correct adjective forms in the table.

| Most one-syllable adjectives | Add **-er**: *old – older, cheap – cheaper, short – (1)* _____
 e.g. *Other e-readers are cheaper than the Reader Plus.* |
| One-syllable adjectives ending in -e | Add **-r** : *nice – nicer, safe – (2)* _____
 e.g. *Your mobile is nicer than mine.* |

HOME (w)

98

One-syllable adjectives ending in consonant-vowel-consonant	Double the final consonant and add -er: thin – thinner, hot – hotter, big – (3) _____
	e.g. This e-reader is smaller/bigger than that one.
Two-syllable adjectives ending in -y	Change the y to i and add -er: happy – happier, funny – funnier, pretty – (4) _____
	e.g. His photo is funnier than hers.
Adjectives with two or more syllables	Form the comparative with more/less
	expensive – more/less expensive, versatile – more/less versatile, interesting – (5) _____
	e.g. The Reader Plus is more expensive than other e-readers.
Irregular adjectives	bad – worse, good – (6) _____
	e.g. Tom's e-reader is worse than this one.

C PRACTISE Complete these sentences with the correct comparative form of the adjective in brackets + than.

1 This laptop is _____ (versatile) mine.
2 Your furniture is _____ (nice) your neighbours' furniture.
3 Shopping online is _____ (easy) going to the shops.
4 My mobile phone is _____ (up-to-date) yours.
5 These jeans are _____ (good) those.
6 Mike's old MP3 player is _____ (big) his new one.

WHAT'S RIGHT?

○ This TV is smaller than that one.
○ This TV is more nicer than that one.
○ This TV is expensiver than that one.
○ This TV is more expensive than that one.

D NOW YOU DO IT Work in pairs. Which of these two types of computer do you prefer and why? Use the words below.

practical   attractive   compact
cheap   user-friendly   good   big

A: I like desktop computers because they're easy to use.
B: I don't. They're a lot bigger than laptops, and you can't carry them around.

WRITING: compound sentences page 75

We can use *and*, *or* and *but* to connect two short sentences. This is called a compound sentence. Use *and* to add extra information, use *but* to add contrasting information and use *or* to show different options.

A In your notebook, connect these sentences using *or*, *and* or *but*.

1 This furniture shop is nice. It's expensive.
2 These trousers are ugly. They're very short.
3 Do you want to try on these shoes? Do you want to try on those ones?
4 My computer is new. It's very slow.
5 This mobile phone is attractive. It's user-friendly.
6 We can watch this film. We can listen to that new CD.

B Choose gadgets (mobile phone, radio, MP3 player, etc) that you own. In your notebook, write three compound sentences about them using *and*, *or* and *but*.

C Find someone in your class who owns similar items. Talk about why your gadgets are different.

A: My laptop is smaller than yours and it's white.
B: Yes, but my laptop is more up-to-date than yours.

LifeSkills

MAKING CHOICES

- Understand the situation.
- Decide what your criteria are.
- Make a choice.

A Read the emails and notes to an office manager. Then write one sentence that summarises his situation.

Jason

The Accounts Dept printer isn't working – AGAIN! We definitely need a new one!

Sally

Hi, Jason. We need new furniture here in Sales: a new chair for one rep, and I need a new desk. This desk is so small! Can we discuss? Thx.

Becky

To: jkelly
From: smartineau
Subject: supplies

Hey, Jason. Can you please get these things for the CEO's office? A nice chair and a new printer. Thanks!

To: bleonard
From: jkelly
Subject: authorisation for office supplies

Hi, Barbara. Everyone needs office supplies this month! The total cost of the things we need is about £1,000. Can you please authorise that amount? Thanks!

To: jkelly
From: bleonard
Subject: Re: authorisation for office supplies

Hi, Jason. Our office supplies expenses are 40% higher than last year, so we really need to spend less. I can authorise £800 at this time, but no more. Sorry!

B Work in pairs. Tick (✓) in the list below what is important for Jason to consider when he orders office supplies.

- ☐ who/which department needs the supplies (Is every department or person equal?)
- ☐ which supplies are more urgent than others (Does he need to get everything now?)
- ☐ the way the person asks for the supplies (polite, impolite, etc)
- ☐ the cost of each item
- ☐ the quality of each item and the amount of money he can spend
- ☐ the design and colour of each item

C Work in pairs, Look at the website on the next page and decide which items Jason needs to order. Make a list with the headings in the box. Then add up the total of all the items. It has to be £800 or less!

Item	Quantity	Cost per unit	Total

PRINTERS & COPIERS

All-in-one printer, copier, scanner
High capacity office quality

£280

All-in-one printer, copier, scanner
Ideal for home / small office

£170

Basic printer
(colour / black & white)

£90

OFFICE CHAIRS

The Boss
£350

Comfort Zone
£205

Office Companion
£120

DESKS

The Executive
Extra large size
Solid wood

£1,230

The L-Desk
Desk + filing cabinets
Wood veneer

£830

Office Mate
Various colours
MDF and wood veneer

£340

PRINTER/COPIER PAPER (PACK OF 500 SHEETS)

High-quality white bond	£6.50	Standard office (35% recycled paper)	£3.59
Letter-quality bond	£4.75	Economy	£2.75
		Special offer: 100 business cards	
		(one colour, same text for all 100)	£10

D Work with another pair. Explain your choices.

HOW TO SAY IT

Evaluating

We can't buy this ... because it's really expensive.

*I think this ... is nicer / better / more practical than the other ...
(and it's less expensive).*

*This ... is better than that one for the CEO / reps / Sales
department.*

What do you think about this ... for ...?

Making a choice

Let's buy this ... for the Sales department and that ... for the CEO.

I want these ... because they're cheaper than those ones.

This ... is definitely better than that ...

*Why don't we get the ... now because it's urgent. We can get the
... later in the year.*

REFLECT ... How can the skill
of making choices be useful to you
in **Self and Society** and **Study and
Learning**?

Language wrap-up

A Look at the pictures and complete the text with the correct clothing words. (5 points)

You should buy your sister clothes – a (1) _____ for when it gets cold or a pair of (2) _____ that she can wear to the gym. Get your brother a cool (3) _____. Why don't you buy your mum a really nice (4) _____ or a (5) _____? Something she can wear in the summer.

B Complete the rest of the text with words from the box. (5 points)

> expensive   user-friendly   powerful   cheap   attractive

You can buy your dad a new mobile phone. They're really (1) _____ now. You can get a good one for only €60. Find one that's (2) _____. You know – nice to look at. Buy your grandmother a camera. Something (3) _____ – she's not good with technology, so it needs to be simple to operate. Why don't you buy your grandfather a telescope? He loves astronomy. Get a (4) _____ one so that he can see a long way. Be careful though – some telescopes can be very (5) _____ – the best ones are over €700!

> **8 – 10 correct:** I can talk about clothes and use adjectives to describe gadgets.
>
> **0 – 7 correct:** Look again at the Vocabulary sections on pages 94 and 96.
>
> SCORE: /10

Read these conversations. Choose the correct options. Complete the sentences with the correct comparative form of the adjective in brackets. (10 points)

1 A: Do you like (1) this / these shoes, Debbie?
   B: Yes, but they're really expensive. Look, those red ones are (2) _____ (nice) and they're (3) _____ (expensive), too.
2 A: Hi, Sally. Look at (4) this / these watch. It's a present from Tony.
   B: Wow – I love it. It's much (5) _____ (good) than my watch!
3 A: Hey, Allison. Do you like (6) these / those bags over there?
   B: Yes, they're nice. I like the small one. It's (7) _____ (pretty) than the big one. And it's (8) _____ (easy) to carry. Let's buy it for Mum's birthday!
4 A: Hey, Anna. Do you see (9) that / those man at the table? He's teaching our maths class today.
   B: Oh, good. I hope he's (10) _____ (interesting) than our usual teacher.

> **8 – 10 correct:** I can use this, that, these, those to clarify what I am talking about and comparative adjectives to compare things.
>
> **0 – 7 correct:** Look again at the Grammar sections on pages 94 and 98.
>
> SCORE: /10

A Complete the conversation with the correct questions from the box.

Can I try it on?   How much is it?   Can I help you?   How is it?   Have you got this shirt in a smaller size?
Have you got it in green?   How would you like to pay?

Shop assistant:	Hi. _____
Customer:	Yes, please. _____
Shop assistant:	Yes, here's a medium.
Customer:	Thanks. _____
Shop assistant:	Of course. There's the fitting room.
Shop assistant:	_____
Customer:	It fits perfectly. _____
Shop assistant:	It's €12.
Customer:	That's fine. _____
Shop assistant:	No, sorry, only in blue.
Customer:	OK, I'll take it.
Shop assistant:	_____
Customer:	With my debit card, please.

B Look back at the conversation and find the following things.

*   a question to offer help
*   two questions asking for different items
*   a request to try an item
*   a question about price
*   a question about payment

C Work in pairs. Imagine that one of you is a shop assistant and the other is a customer. Roleplay a conversation with your partner.

HOW ARE YOU DOING?

Think about your speaking. Do you feel confident using:
○ questions to offer or ask for help in a shop?
○ questions to ask how much something costs?
○ responses to questions in shops?
How do you feel about your speaking generally?

●   ●   ●
Very confident   Not sure…   Need to practise

UNIT 9 LET'S EAT

IN THIS UNIT YOU

- learn language for talking about and ordering food and for making and responding to invitations
- leave formal and informal phone messages
- scan restaurant ads to find information quickly
- listen to and write down phone messages
- write opinions of restaurants to post on websites
- make a plan for a special meal
- ▶ watch a video about different restaurants

SPEAKING
using phone language

Do you usually use formal or informal language when on the phone? What are the differences between formal and informal phone language in your language?

READING
scanning for specific information

In what types of texts do you usually need to find specific information? What kinds of information do you usually look for?

LIFE SKILLS

SELF & SOCIETY

making a plan Why is a plan useful? In what kinds of situations do you need to make a plan? What are people planning in this unit?

A What does food mean to you? Tick (✓) the phrase that you most associate with food.

an adventure ☐

a necessity ☐

B Carry out a class survey. How many people chose each phrase? Discuss the different ways these phrases can relate to food.

A: I think food is an adventure. I like trying foods from different countries.

B: Yes, and I like experimenting when I cook. It's exciting.

C: For me, eating is definitely a social activity. I like to enjoy food with friends and family. It doesn't matter that it's not exciting.

HOW TO SAY IT

Expressing opinions
(Well,) I think/believe (that) …
For me, …
I would say that …
In my opinion, …

a social activity

A Write these food categories in the correct part of the food chart. Guess the number of recommended servings per day for each category.

> fat, salt, and sugar   protein   fruit and vegetables   carbohydrates   dairy products

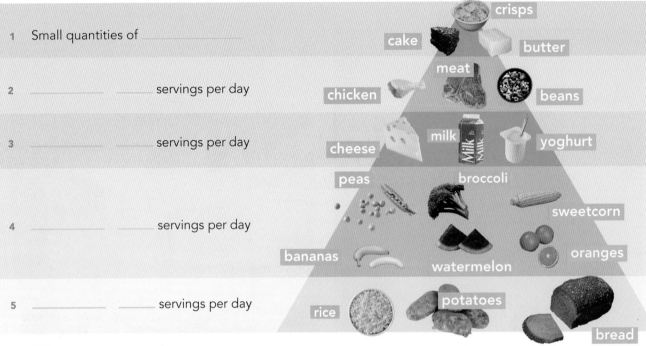

1 Small quantities of _____

2 _____ servings per day

3 _____ servings per day

4 _____ servings per day

5 _____ servings per day

B 🗣 Work in groups. Talk about your diet. Who has the healthiest diet?

A: *Sandra, do you eat a lot of vegetables?*
B: *Not really, but I eat lots of fruit. I love apples and melon!*

A LANGUAGE IN CONTEXT Read these people's comments. Then choose T (true) or F (false) for the sentences below.

Charlie: Can I make a sandwich? We don't have much ham but we have a lot of cheese and tomatoes.

William: We don't have many potatoes, but we have lots of rice and meat. And we have some vegetables.

Lisa: How many apples are there? I want to make a pie. And is there any sugar?

Anne: How much bread do we have? I want some toast. Oh, we don't have any butter!

> **NOTICE!**
> Which words refer to quantities? <u>Underline</u> them.

1 Charlie is making a sandwich with a lot of ham. T / F
2 William is planning to have meat, potatoes and vegetables for dinner. T / F
3 Lisa needs apples and sugar to make a pie. T / F
4 Anne can't have butter on her toast. T / F

B ANALYSE: COUNTABLE AND UNCOUNTABLE NOUNS Read the texts in Exercise A again.

Form Choose the correct option for each rule. Then write *C* (countable) or *U* (uncountable) after each food item in the box.

1 Countable nouns are nouns that you can / can't count. They have / don't have a singular and a plural form.

e.g. apple   apples

 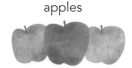

2 Uncountable nouns are nouns that you can / can't count. They have / don't have a plural form.

e.g. rice

| ham _____ | cheese _____ | tomatoes _____ | potatoes _____ | rice _____ | vegetables _____ |
| apples _____ | pie _____ | sugar _____ | bread _____ | toast _____ | butter _____ |

ANALYSE: QUANTIFIERS Read the texts in Exercise A again.

Function Choose the correct option for each rule.

1 We use *a* or *an* to refer to specific / general quantities.
2 We use *some, any, much* and *many* to refer to specific / general quantities.

Form Complete the sentences in the table with *a, an, some, any, much* and *many*. Then choose the correct option to complete the sentences.

a / an / some / any

	Singular countable nouns	Plural countable nouns	Uncountable nouns
Affirmative	I want (1) _____ apple.	I want (4) _____ apples.	I want (7) _____ rice.
Negative	I don't want (2) _____ potato.	I don't want (5) _____ potatoes.	I don't want (8) _____ bread.
Questions	Do you want (3) _____ tomato?	Are there (6) _____ tomatoes?	Do we have (9) _____ butter?

much / many

	Plural Countable nouns	Uncountable nouns
Negative	There aren't (10) _____ vegetables.	There isn't (12) _____ butter.
Questions	How (11) _____ oranges are there? There aren't many tomatoes.	How (13) _____ ham is there? There isn't much bread.

14 Use _____ before singular countable nouns.
   a) *a* or *an*   b) *some*

15 _____ *a* or *an* before uncountable nouns.
   a) Use   b) Do not use

16 We can use *some, any* and *much* before _____ .
   a) plural countable nouns.   b) uncountable nouns.

17 We can use *some, any* and *many* before _____ .
   a) plural countable nouns.   b) uncountable nouns.

18 We use _____ in negatives and questions.
   a) *some*   b) *any*

C PRACTISE Choose the correct option to complete the sentences.

1 Do you want a / an / – apple?
2 I don't want any biscuit / biscuits.
3 Do we have much milk / milks?
4 I want a / some rice with my chicken.
5 Is there any / many ice cream in the fridge?
6 I want some ham / hams.
7 There isn't much / many butter in the fridge.
8 How much / many oranges do we need?

D NOW YOU DO IT Work in groups. Ask and answer questions about the food in your house.

A: *Do you have any vegetables in your house?*
B: *Yes, we have some peas, some sweetcorn and a lot of broccoli.*

A Read the two messages. What is each message about?

1

While you were out
Caller: Dan
Day: Thurs
Time: 10.15
Message: lunch at John's Burgers, 2.30

2

Ryan — message from Lauren
dinner, Fri 13th.
Call her.

B 🎧 **51** Listen to the two phone calls. Underline the incorrect information in each message in Exercise A.

C 🎧 **52** Listen to another phone call and write the message.

3

While you were out
Caller: Eric
Day: Fri
Time: 5.30
Message:

When speaking on the phone, it's important to think about whether the conversation is formal or informal so that you can use the correct language.

A 🎧 **53** Listen to the two conversations below. Which is formal and which is informal?

1 A: Good afternoon, Food for Fun.
   B: Hello. Could I speak to Linda Jenkins, please?
   A: I'm sorry, she isn't here right now. Would you like to leave a message?
   B: Yes. Please ask her to call Helen Glover. My number is 640 806 9271.
   A: Yes, of course.
   B: Thank you.
   A: You're welcome.

2 A: Hello?
   B: Hi, is Olivia there?
   A: No, sorry, she isn't.
   B: Oh, OK. Can I leave a message?
   A: Sure.
   B: This is Mark. Can you ask her to call me?
   A: OK, no problem.
   B: Thanks.

B Underline examples of formal and informal language in the conversations in Exercise A.

C Work in pairs. Follow the instructions below.
- Student A, 'call' Student B and leave a message for another classmate. Student B, write down the message. Switch roles.
- Student A, 'call' Student B and leave a message for your teacher. Student B, you are an office assistant at the school. Write down the message. Switch roles.

GRAMMAR: verb phrases

A 🎧 **54 LANGUAGE IN CONTEXT** Listen to the
conversation below. Why can't Jane go out tonight?

Paul: So, <u>would you like to go out</u> for dinner tonight?
Jane: Well, I'd love to, but I can't.
Paul: Why not?
Jane: Because <u>I have to study</u>. I have a really important maths
test tomorrow and <u>I want to get</u> a good mark.
Paul: Oh, OK, no problem. Well, <u>do you want to have</u> dinner
tomorrow night then?
Jane: Sure. <u>Let's try</u> that new Italian restaurant.
Paul: OK. <u>I'd like to try</u> it, too. <u>I need to go</u> to the gym first, so
<u>shall we meet</u> at, maybe, seven thirty?
Jane: Seven thirty is fine. See you tomorrow!
Paul: OK, bye.

NOTICE!
Look at the <u>underlined</u> phrases.
Which two phrases don't involve
an infinitive (*to* + base form)?

B ANALYSE Look at the <u>underlined</u> phrases in Exercise A.

Function Complete the table with words from the conversation.

Expressing wishes and desires	Making invitations	Making suggestions	Expressing obligation and necessity
I (1) *LET'S* try it. I (2) *love to* get a good mark. I (3) *I WOULD LIKE TO* (but I can't).	*WOULD YOU LIKE* (4) *I WANT to* go out for dinner tonight? (5) _____ want to have dinner tomorrow night?	(6) *SHALL* we meet at seven thirty? (7) *LET'S* try that new Italian restaurant.	I (8) *I HAVE* go to the gym first. I (9) *HAVE* study.

Form Choose the correct options.

1   What form of the verb is used after *would like, love, have, need*
and *want*?
    a)   infinitive (*to* + base form)   b)   base form

2   What form of the verb is used after *let's*?
    a)   infinitive (*to* + base form)   b)   base form

3   What person do we use after *shall*?
    a)   *I* and *we*   b)   *you, he/she/it* and *they*

4   What word does the *'d* in *I'd* represent?
    a)   *had*   b)   *would*

WHAT'S RIGHT?
○ Do you like to go out
tonight?
○ Would you like to go out
tonight?
○ Would you like go out
tonight?
○ Would you love to go out
tonight?

C PRACTISE Complete the conversation with phrases from Exercise B. In some cases,
there is more than one correct answer.

David: Kirsty, (1) _____ go to the cinema tomorrow night?
Kirsty: Oh, sorry. I (2) _____, but I can't. I (3) _____ work. How about Friday night?
I (4) *WOULD LIKE to* see that new Will Smith film.
David: OK. Sounds good. And (5) *SHALL* have dinner after the film?
Kirsty: Sure. (6) *LET'S* have pizza. I (7) *LET'S* go to the Big Cheese!
David: Great! See you then!

D 🗣 **NOW YOU DO IT** Invite different classmates to do things. Accept or refuse their
invitations. When you refuse, give a reason. When you accept, make suggestions for
places to go and times to meet.

   have dinner   go swimming   go for coffee   go shopping

A: *Would you like to go shopping tomorrow?*
B: *I'd love to, but I have to visit my grandparents.*

VOCABULARY: ordering in a restaurant

A Complete the menu with words from the box.

tart sparkling chicken spaghetti cream salad juice

B 🔊55 Listen to Jenny and Alan at a restaurant. Write the letters in the gaps to complete what they say.

Waiter: Good evening. _____

Jenny: Yes, please. What's the soup of the day?

Waiter: It's tomato and basil soup.

Jenny: OK, _____ And then the grilled fish with rice and peas.

Waiter: And for you, sir?

Alan: _____, and then the roast chicken with potatoes and spinach.

Waiter: Would you like any dressing with your salad, sir?

Alan: Yes, please.

Waiter: _____

Jenny: Just some still water for me.

Alan: _____

Waiter: OK. I'll be right back with your drinks.

a) I'd like the soup, please.
b) And the same for me.
c) Are you ready to order?
d) A green salad to start
e) And what would you like to drink?

C Work in groups. Roleplay ordering in a restaurant. Use the menu.

PRONUNCIATION: weak *to*

A 🔊56 Listen to the conversations below. Circle where you hear W (weak) or S (strong) forms of *to*. Answer the questions.

1	A:	Do you want to watch a DVD?	W / S
	B:	I'd love to.	W / S
2	A:	Would you like to go out tonight?	W / S
	B:	I'd love to.	W / S

In short answers when *to* is the last word, is it strong or weak? _____

In phrases like *would like to*, *want to*, etc., is *to* strong or weak? _____

B 🔊57 Work in pairs. Practise this conversation. Listen and check.

A: Would you like to have dinner?
B: I'd like to, but I'm not hungry right now.
A: Do you want to go for a walk first?
B: Yes, I'd love to.

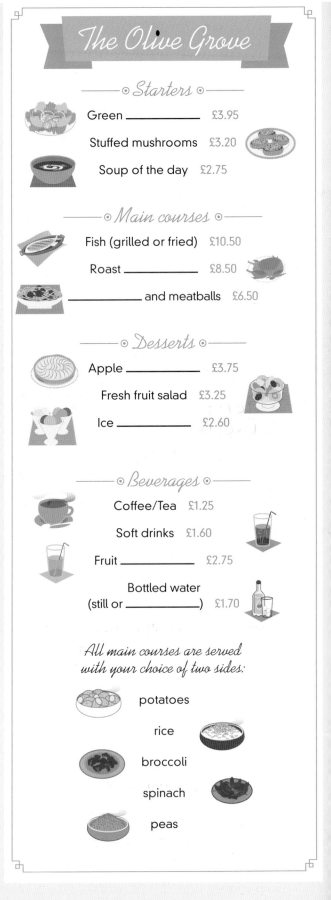

The Olive Grove

— ⊙ *Starters* ⊙ —

Green _____ £3.95

Stuffed mushrooms £3.20

Soup of the day £2.75

— ⊙ *Main courses* ⊙ —

Fish (grilled or fried) £10.50

Roast _____ £8.50

_____ and meatballs £6.50

— ⊙ *Desserts* ⊙ —

Apple _____ £3.75

Fresh fruit salad £3.25

Ice _____ £2.60

— ⊙ *Beverages* ⊙ —

Coffee/Tea £1.25

Soft drinks £1.60

Fruit _____ £2.75

Bottled water
(still or _____) £1.70

All main courses are served with your choice of two sides:

potatoes

rice

broccoli

spinach

peas

To find specific information in a text, don't read every word. Look at the text quickly to find the words or numbers that give you the information.

A Read about this situation. <u>Underline</u> the important information.

You and your friends want to have dinner late on Saturday because you are going to the theatre first. You don't want to make a reservation. One of your friends is a strict vegetarian.

B Scan the ads and find the best restaurant for the situation.

AMBER

Fine international food in an intimate atmosphere

Extensive vegetarian menu

HOURS:
Tuesday–Friday, 11.30am–11pm
Saturday, 11.30am–1am
Closed Monday

Reservations required on weekends

CALL
0213 6746211

189 Parliament Hill

Gourmet Burgers

Most original burgers, with a gourmet twist!

Try our speciality vegetarian burgers!
• Live music Friday & Saturday nights
• Family-style seating

Hours:
Mon–Thurs, 11am–10pm
Fri & Sat, 11am–2am
61 Regent's Square, WC1 6LT
Tel: 0217 9361187

No reservations necessary

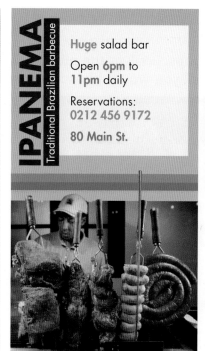

IPANEMA
Traditional Brazilian barbecue

Huge salad bar

Open **6pm** to **11pm** daily

Reservations:
0212 456 9172

80 Main St.

Large variety of mixed drinks

Open daily from **11am** to **9pm**

47 Florence Road, SE1

0218 327 8854

C Read the ad for the restaurant you chose in Exercise B. Find the information below as quickly as you can. <u>Underline</u> each item.

• the type of food • entertainment • the phone number • the location

D  Work in groups. Discuss these questions.

1 Do you prefer eating out or eating at home? Why?
2 What are your favourite kinds of restaurants?
3 What kinds of restaurants don't you like?

HOW TO SAY IT

I like vegetarian/seafood/Italian restaurants.

I don't like noisy/quiet restaurants.

I prefer restaurants with traditional food/ live music.

A Read the blog. What two things does the writer like about the restaurant?

Name: Rasta Reggae
Location: Barnes Road

Rasta Reggae is a Caribbean-style restaurant and music club. The prices are a bit high, but the food is excellent. Try the spicy grilled prawns or the Jamaican jerk chicken with rice and peas. There is a very good reggae band on Friday and Saturday nights.

Posted by Michelle on 3rd July

Home

Login

Register

Help

Contact

Add comment | Email

B Write a blog entry in your notebook like the one in Exercise A.

C Work in groups. Read each other's blog entries. Discuss these questions.

1 Which of the restaurants in the blog entries do you know? Do you agree with the blog entry? Why or why not?
2 Which of the restaurants would you like to try? Why?

Let's eat UNIT 9 **111**

LifeSkills

MAKING A PLAN

- Make a list of the things you need to do.
- Write the things you need to do in a logical order.
- Add specific details to each thing on your list.

A Work in groups. Look at the photos of two styles of meal. Decide which style of meal you would like to make for a group meal and why.

A: *I'd like to make meal A because it's more elegant.*
B: *Really? I'd like to make meal B. It's less formal and more fun!*

B Now decide on the most logical order for planning the meal and number the steps.

- [ ] Decide what dishes to have. Include drinks, starters and desserts.
- [ ] Decide how much money you can spend.
- [ ] Decide what kind of meal you want (formal or informal).
- [ ] Decide when and where to have the meal.
- [ ] Check to see if anyone in the group doesn't eat certain foods.
- [ ] Make a shopping list. Include ingredients for the dishes and things you need apart from food, e.g. ice.
- [ ] On the day, get together to prepare your meal, and have fun!

C Complete the notes for planning the meal.

Chef Ollie's
PLAN FOR MEAL

Date: _____

Place: _____

Number of people: _____

▼ **Style:**

Guests at table ☐   Buffet ☐   Picnic ☐

Barbecue ☐   Other: _____

Budget:

_____

▼ Food and drinks

Appetisers

_____

Starter

_____

Main course

_____

Dessert

_____

Drinks

_____

▼ Things to buy:

Prepared food / drinks

_____

Ingredients for
dishes to prepare

_____

Other things

_____

D   Make a copy of your meal plan on a piece of paper. Put your plan on the wall. Read other groups' plans. Which plan is your favourite?

REFLECT ... How can the skill of making a plan be useful to you in **Work and Career** and **Study and Learning**?

Language wrap-up

1 VOCABULARY

Complete the conversation with words from the box. (10 points)

> green   dessert   mushrooms   sparkling   soup   chocolate   tart   bread   fried   salad

Waiter: Good evening. Are you ready to order?

Bruno: Yes. I'd like the (1) _____ of the day to start and then the roast chicken, please.

Valerie: I'd like the stuffed (2) _____ to start and then the fish.

Waiter: Would you like the fish grilled or (3) _____?

Valerie: Um, grilled, please.

Waiter: OK. Would you like any (4) _____ or vegetables?

Bruno: Yes, please. I'd like a (5) _____ salad without any dressing.

Valerie: And I'd like potatoes and broccoli. We'd like a bottle of (6) _____ water, too.

Bruno: Oh, and I'd like some (7) _____ and butter, please.

Waiter: OK, I'll be right back.

Bruno: So, do you think you'd like to have (8) _____ later?

Valerie: Yes, I'd like to try some apple (9) _____ or maybe the (10) _____ cake.

> **8 – 10 correct:** I can talk about food and order food in a restaurant.
> **0 – 7 correct:** Look again at the Vocabulary sections on pages 106 and 110.
> **SCORE:**   /10

2 GRAMMAR

A   Complete the email with phrases from the box. (5 points)

> I need to get up   Would you like to come   I have to go   I'd like to cook   shall we watch

Hi Leah! How are you? I'm at work. (1) _____ to my flat for dinner tonight? (2) _____ something really nice, and I don't want to eat alone! Can you bring something to drink, and maybe something for dessert? Oh, and (3) _____ a film after dinner, too? I can't go to bed too late, though – (4) _____ early tomorrow for a meeting. Anyway, (5) _____ now. I have a lot to do. Call me later – hope to see you tonight. Love, Suzy

B   Choose the correct options to complete Leah's answer. (5 points)

Sure! That sounds good, Suzy. Let's have (1) some / any ice cream for dessert. Shall I bring a starter too? We can have (2) a / some cheese and (3) olive / olives before dinner. Do you have (4) any / many cheese? Oh, and don't cook steak, OK? I'm not eating (5) much / many meat these days, but fish is fine! See you later! Leah

> **8 – 10 correct:** I can use countable and uncountable nouns and verb phrases to talk about plans, invitations, suggestions and obligations.
> **0 – 7 correct:** Look again at the Grammar sections on pages 106 and 109.
> **SCORE:**   /10

WRITING WORKSHOP

A Read the two reviews of a restaurant. Which one is mostly positive? Which is mostly negative?

B <u>Underline</u> the positive comments in both reviews. (Circle) the negative comments.

C Write P (mostly positive) or N (mostly negative) after each statement.

1 The roast chicken is terrible! _____
2 They have a lot of different things on the menu to choose from. _____
3 The desserts are homemade and very fresh. _____
4 The décor isn't very nice. _____
5 The food is pretty good, but it's really expensive. _____
6 There are great bands at the weekend. _____
7 I don't recommend the steak, but in general the food is great. _____
8 You have to shout because the music is really loud. _____

Food for Thought...

Cindyg1:

Don't go to Hawaii Waves if you're really hungry! The service is very slow, and the portions are small. The food is OK, but nothing special, and it really isn't very Hawaiian. The drinks are good, and the Hawaiian décor and surfing music are fun. It's a good place just for drinks, but not for dinner.

Ray45:

Hawaii Waves is a fun restaurant with pretty good food. They don't have many things on the menu, but the teriyaki tuna is excellent! The drinks are a bit expensive, but they have a lot of great cocktails.

D Think of a restaurant in your area. Write your impressions of it.

NAME OF RESTAURANT:
[   ]

LOCATION:
[   ]

TYPE OF FOOD:
[   ]

PRICES:
Low [ ]   Average [ ]   High [ ]

ENTERTAINMENT:
Yes [ ]   No [ ]

Positive impressions	Negative impressions

E Write a comment for a blog about local restaurants in your notebook.

HOW ARE YOU DOING?

Look back at your writing and tick the statements that are true.
○ It is clear whether I have a mostly positive or mostly negative opinion of the restaurant.
○ My blog gives several reasons for my positive or negative opinion.
Now ask your partner to look at your writing and tick.
Is it clear whether the writer has a mostly positive or mostly negative opinion of the restaurant?

● Well done!   ● Nearly!   ● Think again!

UNIT 10 SPEAKING OF THE PAST

IN THIS UNIT YOU

- ⚙ learn language for talking about past experiences and events
- ⚙ listen to conversations about past experiences
- ⚙ write connected sentences about something that happened to you recently
- ⚙ read and answer a survey about your past year
- ⚙ tell someone about a past positive or negative experience
- ⚙ make notes on texts about events in the history of different cities around the world
- ▶ watch a video about holidays in different cities

LISTENING
understanding the main idea
Do you always hear every word of a conversation? How do you understand the conversation if you don't hear every word?

WRITING
sequencing and connecting ideas
When you write or talk about an event or experience, how do you usually order your ideas?

LIFE SKILLS

STUDY & LEARNING

making notes on a text
What reasons do people make notes on a text?

A Tick (✓) the photos that represent activities you did in the past month.

B Count the boxes you ticked and look at your score below.

0–2 Are you bored? Try to have more fun!
3–5 A nice balance!
6–7 Whoa! Make sure you take time to relax too!

C 🗣 Talk to your partner. How many ticks does he/she have?

A: *How many ticks do you have?*
B: *I have three. It's a nice balance.*
   How about you?
A: *I have six!*
B: *Whoa! Try to relax, too!*

HOW TO SAY IT 🗣

Discussing results

How many ticks …?   Try to …
How/What about you?   You need to …
Make sure you …

GRAMMAR: past simple – affirmative statements

A LANGUAGE IN CONTEXT Read the tour evaluation below. Answer the questions.

1 Is Julie and Max's evaluation good or bad in general?
2 Do they mention any problems?

WORLD TOUR SERVICE

PLEASE TAKE A FEW MINUTES TO WRITE A SHORT EVALUATION OF YOUR TOUR WITH US.

We took a tour to Ireland, and we had a fantastic time. WTS planned our trip very carefully and we visited a lot of places. We especially liked Dublin. It's an amazing city! The tour guides explained everything very clearly, and they answered all of our questions. They knew a lot about Irish history. They were also very helpful, and they carried our heavy bags for us. The hotel in Cork was a bit uncomfortable, but in general, we stayed in very nice hotels. We loved Ireland, and we'd like to go back.

JULIE WEST AND MAX RUSHMORE

NOTICE!
Look at the past simple verbs in blue. What is the ending of most past simple verbs in English?

B ANALYSE Read the text in Exercise A again.

Function Choose the correct option to complete the sentence.
We use the past simple to talk about …

a) events in the past.   b) events that began in the past and are still happening at the moment of speaking.

Form Complete the table with the correct past simple verb forms.

Regular verbs		Irregular verbs	
Base form	Past simple form	Base form	Past simple form
explain	(1) _____	be	(5) _____
like	(2) _____	have	(6) _____
carry	(3) _____	know	(7) _____
plan	(4) _____	take	(8) _____

The complete list of irregular verbs is on page 168.

Spelling rules for simple past regular verbs:
- Most verbs, add **-ed**: explain – explain**ed**
- Verbs ending in -e, add **-d**: love – love**d**
- Verbs ending in consonant + y, change -y to **-i** and add **-ed**: carry – carr**ied**
- One-syllable verbs ending in one vowel + one consonant, double the consonant and add **-ed**: plan – plann**ed**

C PRACTISE Complete the email with the past simple of the verbs in brackets.

To: tracy_smith@mymail.com
From: robert_brown@mymail.com
Subject: Tanzania!

Hey, Tracy! Last month Susan and I (1) _____ (go) on a tour in Tanzania, and it (2) _____ (be) incredible! We (3) _____ (travel) from the town of Arusha to a volcanic crater called Ngorongoro. We (4) _____ (stay) in a cabin near the crater, and the first evening we (5) _____ (watch) the sunset over the volcano – wow! The next day we walked into the crater, and we (6) _____ (see) lots of wild animals, including zebras, elephants, and lions! I (7) _____ (take) lots of photos! Our guide (8) _____ (explain) the geology of the crater, and he also (9) _____ (tell) us about the people and the animals in the region. We (10) _____ (have) a great time!

D NOW YOU DO IT
Work in groups. Talk about the last trip you took.

My family/friends and I went to …
We stayed at … It was …

Time expressions:
yesterday
last Tuesday/week/month/year
three hours/days/weeks/ months/years ago
in March/2010

PRONUNCIATION: -ed endings

A ▶58 Listen to the sounds in the table. Then listen to the past simple forms of the verbs in the box and write them in the correct columns in the table.

listened watched decided wanted played liked	/d/	/t/	/ɪd/

B ▶59 Work in pairs. Listen and repeat the verb pairs. Then listen again and write the past simple forms in the correct columns in the table above.

READING: a survey

A Read the first paragraph of the article. What is the topic of the survey?

a) readers' birthdays   b) readers' email use   c) readers' experiences

HOW WAS YOUR YEAR?

It's Your Life emailed 100 readers on their birthdays and asked them how they felt about the past year of their lives. Then they completed a survey about specific positive experiences during the year. Many people were surprised at the results! For example, a lot of people who said, 'It was OK,' really had a fantastic year, according to the survey. Sometimes we focus too much on the bad or boring things in our lives! Now you try it …

My past year was …
a) great!   b) OK.   c) not very good.
Now circle yes or no for each statement about your past year.

1 I took an interesting or fun trip.	YES NO	**6** I did a lot of exercise or sports.	YES NO
2 I went to some great parties.	YES NO	**7** I discovered some great music.	YES NO
3 I met some new friends.	YES NO	**8** I read some good books.	YES NO
4 I had a romantic relationship.	YES NO	**9** I got a new pet.	YES NO
5 I went out with my friends a lot.	YES NO	**10** I tried a new hobby.	YES NO

Now look at your score.

Every 'yes' equals 1 point and every 'no' equals 0 points. Does your general opinion of your past year match your score?

6–10 It looks like you had a great year!
3–5 Your year was fun! But maybe you can do more …
0–2 Why not try some more of the things on the list?

B Read the whole survey and choose T (true) or F (false) for these sentences.

1 The magazine asked the readers how they felt about the previous month.   T / F
2 The survey was about positive experiences.   T / F
3 Lots of people were surprised by the results.   T / F
4 People who say their year was 'OK' are often right.   T / F
5 Four statements in the survey relate to hobbies and activities.   T / F
6 Four statements in the survey relate to relationships and socialising.   T / F

C Now complete the survey for yourself.

D Carry out a class survey. Answer these questions.

1 How many people in the class did each thing on the survey?
2 How many people had a great year?
3 How many people were surprised by the results?

VOCABULARY: adjectives with -ed and -ing

A Read the examples. Answer the questions.

A: Do you think this film is interesting?   A: Are you interested in this film?
B: No. It's boring.   B: No. I'm bored.

1 Which adjectives refer to the film? What is the ending on the adjectives?
2 Which adjectives refer to the person who is watching the film? What is the ending on the adjectives?

B Check that you know the meanings of the adjective pairs in the message. Then choose the correct options to complete the message.

New Message

To: Rachel   WERE

Hi Rachel,
We had a great weekend in Prague! It's an amazing / amazed city! We saw some traditional polka dancers, and I loved them, but Sam isn't very interesting / interested in folk music. Poor Sam – he was boring / bored! But we also went on a boat on the Vltava River, and that was really exciting / excited! We walked all around the historic district, and it was very interesting / interested. We were pretty tiring / tired on Sunday night, but it was fun.
Love, Ellie
P.S. Here are a few photos of Prague!

C 🗣 Work in pairs. Talk about these topics. Use -ed and -ing adjectives.

- the last film you saw
- your last holiday
- the last sports event you went to

A: *Last month I went to a football match. It was really exciting.*
B: *Really? I watched a golf competition on TV last night, but it was kind of boring.*

WHAT'S RIGHT?

The party was boring. =
◯ I was bored there.
⊙ I was boring there.

GRAMMAR: past simple – questions and negative statements

A 🎧 60 LANGUAGE IN CONTEXT Listen to the conversation below. Did Gary and Monica have fun last weekend?

Gary: Hey, Monica. How was your weekend?
Monica: It wasn't very good. I went dancing with some friends on Saturday night, but I didn't feel well. I didn't have fun at all. I didn't do anything on Sunday, it was a boring day. What about you? What did you do this weekend?
Gary: Oh, I didn't do much. Let's see, on Friday night I stayed at home and watched TV. I had to work on Saturday, but I went out on Saturday night. Phoebe and I tried that new Italian restaurant on Bridge Street.
Monica: Oh, yeah? Did you like it?
Gary: It was OK, nothing special. Then on Sunday I played basketball.
Monica: Oh, was it a good game?
Gary: No, it wasn't. My team lost.
Monica: Well, next weekend has to be better!

B ANALYSE Read the conversation in Exercise A again.

Form Write the missing words in the table. Then choose the correct option to complete the sentence below.

NOTICE!
Find and (circle) the past simple verbs in the conversation in Exercise A. Say which verb you think each past simple form belongs to, e.g. **was** – the verb **be.**

	be	Other verbs
Negative statements	It wasn't very good.	I (4) WAS feel well.
Yes/No questions	(1) WAS it a good game?	(5) DID you like it?
Short answers	Yes, it was. / No, (2) _____.	Yes, we did. / No, we didn't.
Information questions	How (3) WAS your weekend?	What (6) DID you DO this weekend?

In negative statements, questions and short answers, use *did* or *didn't* with …
a) be. b) other verbs.

C PRACTISE Complete the questions 1–6. Then match them to the answers a–f.

1 *Did* you go out on Saturday night?
2 Where DID you go?
3 WAS it fun?
4 Who DID you go with?
5 What DID you do on Sunday?
6 How WAS the food?

a) I went to lunch at Whole Earth.
b) I went to a club.
c) Yes, I did.
d) It was excellent!
e) I went with my friends.
f) Yes, it was.

WHAT'S RIGHT?
○ What you did at the weekend?
○ What did you do at the weekend?
○ What were you do at the weekend?

D 🔊 **NOW YOU DO IT** Work in pairs. Ask about your partner's weekend.

A: *Did you go out on Friday?*
B: *No, I didn't. I stayed at home and watched a DVD. What about you?*

LISTENING: understanding the main idea

It isn't necessary to understand every word of a conversation to understand the topic and the main idea. Listen for key words and repeated words.

A 🔊 **61** Listen to the conversations. Choose the topic of each one.

1 a) a holiday b) work c) the man's wife
2 a) a festival b) a trip c) the weekend

B 🔊 **61** Listen again. Choose the main idea of each conversation.

This person had …
1 a) a good time. 2 a) a good time.
   b) a bad time.   b) a bad time.

C 🔊 **61** What key words or repeated words did you hear? Listen again if necessary.

⚙ When we write or talk about an event, we usually tell the story in chronological order. We use specific words and phrases to indicate sequence.

A Read the blog entry. Answer the questions below.

SUPER COOL PETS BL🐾G

Two months ago, I found a dog in the street. First, I asked my neighbours if it was their dog, but it wasn't. Then, I made posters and put them around our village. Nobody called me.

After that, I put an ad in the newspaper. A week later, a man called, but it wasn't his dog. Finally, I decided to keep the dog. His name is Joey, and he's great!

Posted by
Sarah on 20th August

Add comment | email

1 Which words indicate the order of events in the story?
2 What punctuation do we usually use after sequencing words or phrases at the beginning of a sentence?

B Number the sentences in a logical order to form a story. There is more than one correct order!

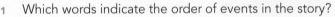

- [1] I had an amazing day!
- [5] She had tickets for a concert to see my favourite band that night!
- [6] The concert was amazing.
- [7] ... she really surprised me!
- [2] It was my birthday, and my girlfriend picked me up at my house in the morning.
- [ ] ... we went home at about midnight. It was really an incredible birthday!
- [3] ... we went shopping. She bought me an MP3 player and a jacket.
- [4] ... she took me to a really nice restaurant for lunch.

C Write the story in your notebook. Add sequencing words and time expressions from the box below.

| First   After that   Finally   Then   Two months ago |

D 🗣 Work in pairs. Read your stories. Are they exactly the same? If not, are they both logical?

VOCABULARY: memorable experiences

A Match the verbs and noun phrases below to make collocations for memorable experiences.

a picture of …

see   a famous person

take   a fantastic gift

       a special letter

get   an amazing concert

       a trip to …

B Write sentences that are true for you using the ideas in Exercise A and your own ideas. Add more information.

A year / a week / six months ago,

Once,

Last week / month / year,

In March / 2011,

I   saw …

    took …

    got …

C Work in groups. Compare your sentences in Exercise B.

A: *Once I saw a famous person. I saw George Clooney at the airport.*

B: *Really? Wow!*

SPEAKING: talking about a past experience

A 🎧 62 Listen to the conversation below. Did Sally have a good experience or a bad experience?

Sally: I was on TV three months ago.

Anna: Really? What show were you on?

Sally: My boyfriend and I were on *Dance Craze*.

Anna: Wow! Did you win?

Sally: Yes, we did! We won two thousand pounds!

Anna: Really? That's amazing!

B Think of an experience that happened to you. Write notes about it.

The experience: _____

_____

When it happened: _____

Where it happened: _____

Other information: _____

C 🗣 Work in groups. Talk about your experience. Answer any questions from people in your group.

LifeSkills

MAKING NOTES ON A TEXT

- Read the text to understand the main idea. Don't make notes.
- Read the text again. <u>Underline</u> the important information.
- Write key words and phrases in your notebook. Don't copy complete sentences.
- Reread your notes. Are they logical? Do they help you remember what you read?

A Read the magazine article. Why is the culture of New Orleans different from the culture in other parts of the USA?

New Orleans
SINCE 1718
A CITY WITH A
Different Flavour

The biggest cultural influence in the USA is from Great Britain, but one exception to that is in New Orleans, on the Mississippi River. In the 17th century, the French explorer LaSalle claimed the river for France, and in 1718, the French founded New Orleans. The city became a favourite port for pirates! In 1762, France ceded New Orleans to Spain, but in 1800, Spain returned the city to France. Finally, in 1803, France sold the territory, including New Orleans, to the USA.

Many Americans went to live in New Orleans, but French speakers continued to dominate in the 19th and early 20th centuries. They did not come only from France, but also from Haiti (a former French colony) and from Canada. The French-speaking Canadian immigrants were Acadians (called Cajuns). The French, the Cajun, and the Haitian cultures joined together to create the unique architecture, cuisine, and music that are famous in New Orleans today.

The history of French speakers in New Orleans
17th century – LaSalle claimed Mississippi River for France
1718 – French founded NO
1762 – French gave NO to Spain
1800 – Spain returned NO to France
1803 – France sold NO to USA
19th & early 20th centuries: French speakers from France, Haiti, Canada (Cajuns) dominant

B Read the text again. <u>Underline</u> information that relates to this question: What is the history of French speakers in New Orleans?

C Read the notes. Compare the information in the notes with the information you <u>underlined</u>. Is it the same?

D Work in pairs. Student A, read the question and the text about Dubai. Student B, read the question and the text about Hong Kong.

Student A
How did Dubai become a wealthy city?

Dubai **for** Business

Dubai, on the Arabian Gulf, is an important international centre of finance and tourism. Many people think that Dubai's success is only because of its oil reserves, but oil is only one factor. In the 19th Century, Dubai became a major port and centre of commerce on shipping routes from India. It also had an enormous international market for its pearls. Dubai was already a wealthy city, and the discovery of oil in 1966 made it much, much wealthier.

Sheikh Rashid, Dubai's leader since 1958, used oil money to modernise the infrastructure of Dubai. He made Dubai a free port, and it became the major business centre for the region. Rashid also promoted Dubai as a tourist destination. In the 1970s, Dubai joined with six other emirates to form the United Arab Emirates. The UAE is now one of the richest nations in the world.

Student B
What was the role of Great Britain in the history of Hong Kong?

The British **in** Hong Kong

Before the 19th century, the island of Hong Kong had a very small population. The residents were Chinese fishermen (and a number of pirates!). In 1842, Britain defeated China in a war and took possession of the island of Hong Kong. (The island gets its name from the abundance of flowers that grow there. 'Hong Kong' means 'fragrant harbour'.) In a second war, Britain took Kowloon, across the harbour from Hong Kong. Finally, in 1898, a large area next to Kowloon also became British property. This annexation gave the British more space to expand the colony.

Britain established a major port in Hong Kong, and the city became famous for shipping, banking, and insurance. Many people immigrated to Hong Kong from China in the 20th century. In 1984, Britain agreed to return Hong Kong to China in 1997. On July 1st, 1997, in a big celebration, it officially became part of China. Today Hong Kong is still one of the world's major financial centres.

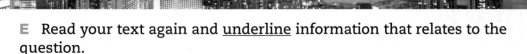

E Read your text again and <u>underline</u> information that relates to the question.

F Use the <u>underlined</u> information in your text to write notes in your notebook. Then read your notes to check that you can understand them.

G   Close your book. Use your notes to tell your partner about the text you read.

A: *What was your question?*
B: *My question was: How did Dubai become a wealthy city?*
A: *So what did you find out?*
B: *Well, Dubai initially became wealthy in the 19th century as …*

? REFLECT … How can the skill of making notes on a text be useful to you in **Self and Society** and **Work and Career**?

Language wrap-up

1 VOCABULARY

Complete the sentences below. Use phrases from the box or choose the correct options. (10 points)

> saw a concert   met a famous person   got a special letter   took a trip   got a fantastic gift

1 I had a great weekend. My friend and I (1) _took a trip_ to Niagara Falls. It was pretty (2) amazed / ~~amazing.~~

2 It was my birthday yesterday. I (3) _got a fantastic letter_ from my parents. They gave me a digital camera. I was really (4) excited / exciting.

3 My husband (5) _got a special letter_ in the post yesterday. It was an invitation to meet the President. He was really (6) surprised / surprising.

4 I had a great weekend. I (7) _saw a concert_ on Saturday night. Manu Chao played in London. The trip was pretty (8) tired / tiring, but it was a fantastic night!

5 I (9) _met a famous person_ once. He is a famous film director. He sat next to me on a flight to Auckland. We talked a lot about film. He was very (10) interested / interesting.

> **8 – 10 correct:** I can talk about memorable experiences and use adjectives with –ed and –ing endings.
> **0 – 7 correct:** Look again at the Vocabulary sections on pages 120 and 123.
> **SCORE:**   /10

2 GRAMMAR

Complete this postcard with the correct past simple form of the verbs in brackets. (10 points)

Cape Town

Hi Jasmine,
Here I am in Cape Town. It's great. The hotel is amazing and the people are really friendly. When I (1) _arrived_ (arrive) at the airport, I (2) _took_ (take) a taxi to the hotel. Then, in the afternoon I (3) _going_ (go) to the top of Table Mountain. The views (4) _____ (be) spectacular! In the evening, I (5) _meeting_ (meet) my friend Amy for dinner. We (6) _having_ (have) a traditional South African barbecue – it was really delicious! I (7) _not staying_ (not stay) out too late, though. I (8) _____ (be) really tired. And how are you? What (9) _do_ you _do_ (do) to celebrate your birthday? Sorry I (10) _____ (not be) there!
Louisa

CAPE TOWN
28.03.13
SOUTH AFRICA
SOUTH AFRICA 95c

Jasmine Brown
35 High Street
London
SW1 6HK
England

> **8 – 10 correct:** I can use the past simple to talk about past events and to ask questions about past events.
> **0 – 7 correct:** Look again at the Grammar sections on pages 118 and 120.
> **SCORE:**   /10

SPEAKING WORKSHOP

A **Number the sentences in this anecdote in the correct order.**

1 I have to tell you about what happened last weekend!

3 The band played for about two hours, and they were great!

2 On Saturday night, I went to a Coldplay concert with some friends.

4 At the end of the concert, an announcer told us to look at our tickets.

6 All of my friends had blue stamps on their tickets, but my ticket had a red stamp.

7 We went backstage, and the announcer introduced us to Coldplay!

5 The announcer said, 'Ten people have a red stamp! Those ten people can come backstage to meet the band!'

8 I met Coldplay! Can you believe it?

B **Look back at the anecdote and answer these questions.**

1 How does the speaker introduce her anecdote?

2 Does the anecdote include a lot of detail?

3 Is the last sentence of the anecdote an event in the story or a comment?

C **Think of an experience that you had. Complete the notes for an anecdote.**

The experience:

When it happened:

Where it happened:

Steps in the story:

1)

D **Work in pairs. Tell your anecdote. Refer to your notes to help you.**

Try to remember to:
- include an introductory sentence.
- put the events of the anecdote in a logical order.
- use the past simple tense to tell the story.
- use sequencing words.

paste tense

E **Now practise telling your anecdote to a new person.**

HOW ARE YOU DOING?

Think about your speaking. Do you feel confident:

◯ using the past simple to tell someone an anecdote?

◯ using sequencing words to order your anecdote logically?

How do you feel about your speaking generally?

●   ●   ●

Very confident   Not sure...   Need to practise

UNIT 11 GREAT LIVES

IN THIS UNIT YOU

- ⚙ learn language for talking about people and events in the past
- ⚙ read biographical information about the life of a famous person
- ⚙ learn how to take time to think when remembering and recounting events
- ⚙ listen to biographical information about the life of a famous person
- ⚙ write a short biography
- ⚙ brainstorm ideas of famous people to write about
- ▶ watch a video about the lives of famous people

READING
scanning for specific information

What kinds of facts do we often want to find quickly when we read biographical texts?

SPEAKING
taking time to think

Why do we sometimes need time to think when we are having a conversation?

LIFE SKILLS

brainstorming in a group What is brainstorming? Why is it a useful skill?

STUDY & LEARNING

A How many of these people do you recognise?
What were their professions?

Luciano Pavarotti

Indira Gandhi

John F Kennedy

Cleopatra

Coco Chanel

Gianni Versace

Martin Luther King

WHY WERE THEY FAMOU

HOW TO SAY IT

Comparing

Cleopatra and Coco Chanel were both …

They both lived/worked/had …

Indira Gandhi, John F Kennedy, and Martin Luther King were all …

They all lived/worked/had …

B Work in pairs. Put the people in Exercise A in different groups or pairs according to their similarities. Think of as many combinations as possible.

Coco Chanel and Gianni Versace were both fashion designers.

A Write the words and phrases from the box under the correct pictures.

retire   graduate   have children   get a job

1   be born

2   grow up

3   GRADUATED.

4   GET A JOB

5   get married

6   HAVE CHIL

7   _____

8   die

B Work in pairs. Tell your partner about a family member's life. Use the past simple form of as many of the expressions in Exercise A as you can.

My grandfather was born in 1940. He grew up in a small town. He graduated from university in 1964 …

LISTENING: to a life story

A 🎧 63 Look at the notes below and think about what information you need to listen for. Then listen to the life story. Do not try to complete the notes yet.

B 🎧 63 Listen again and complete the notes in Exercise A.

Audrey Hepburn

Date of birth: _____

Place of birth: Brussels, Belgium

Profession: _____

Her age when she moved to New York: _____

Year she won her first Oscar: _____

Her last film: Always, with director Steven Spielberg, 1989

Type of work in her later life: Working with UNICEF to

help children.

Date she died: _____

C What other information did you learn about the life of Audrey Hepburn?

A LANGUAGE IN CONTEXT Read the article below.

Why do people remember Steve Irwin?

THE REAL CROCODILE HUNTER

Steve Irwin was a famous conservationist and TV presenter. He was born in Australia in 1962, and he grew up on his parents' wildlife park. Steve loved reptiles, and he got a python for his birthday when he was six years old! When Steve was older, he learnt to work with crocodiles. In 1996, Irwin started his TV show, *The Crocodile Hunter*, and it became popular in many countries. On 4th September, 2006, when Steve went to the Great Barrier Reef to film ocean animals, a stingray stung him. He died that day of cardiac arrest. **People all over the world were sad when Steve Irwin died.** Many people still remember his excellent work in the conservation of endangered species.

WHAT'S RIGHT?

○ When Steve was six years old, he got a python.
○ When Steve was six years old he got a python.
○ Steve got a python, when he was six years old.
○ Steve got a python when he was six years old.

NOTICE!

Look back at the sentence in **bold**. Which action happened first?
a) People were sad.
b) Steve Irwin died.

B ANALYSE Read the sentence in **bold** in the text in Exercise A.

Function Choose the correct option to complete the sentence.
The action in the *when* clause happens … the other event in the sentence.
a) at the same time or before   b) after

Form Look back at the text and underline the sentences with *when*.
Which statements are true? Tick (✓) those which are correct.
a) ☐ *When* clauses always go at the beginning of a sentence.
b) ☐ *When* clauses always go at the end of a sentence.
c) ☐ *When* clauses can go at the beginning or at the end of a sentence.
d) ☐ We always use a comma if a *when* clause comes at the beginning of a sentence.
e) ☐ We never use a comma with *when* clauses.

C PRACTISE Rewrite these sentences, changing the position of the *when* clause.

1 When my friend told me the news, I was surprised.
   I was surprised when my friend told me the news.

2 Sally was happy when she got a new car.

3 I got a puppy when I was ten.

4 When I was little, I loved going to the cinema.

5 People were surprised when my dad got a new job.

6 When I went shopping, I saw my teacher.

7 When our friends arrived, my flatmate was asleep.

8 I called my friend when I arrived at the station.

D NOW YOU DO IT Work in groups. Tell your group about something:
• that happened when you were young.
• you loved when you were little.
• that happened the last time you went out.

When I was young, I broke my arm. I had to go to hospital.

When you come across a slightly more difficult text, try to focus only on the information you need to find out.

A Work in pairs. Student A, scan the first paragraph and complete sentences 1–5. Student B, scan the second paragraph and complete sentences 6–10.

AN **AMERICAN** ICON

The story of the American automobile industry began on 30th July, 1863, when Henry Ford was born on a farm in Michigan. As a boy, Ford did not like school or farm work, but he was interested in mechanical things. In 1879, when Ford was 16, he left home and moved to the city of Detroit. He worked as a machinist there for three years and then returned to his family's farm. On the farm, he operated and repaired steam engines in farm machines. In 1891, he returned to Detroit and got a job as an engineer. He began experimenting with internal combustion engines, and in 1896, he invented a vehicle called the Quadricycle. He experimented with different vehicles for several more years, and in 1903, he started the Ford Motor Company.

Many people think Henry Ford invented the automobile, but he didn't. Gottlieb Daimler and Karl Benz invented vehicles powered by gasoline engines in 1885–1886. Henry Ford actually became famous because he invented the assembly line, in 1913. At the new Ford automobile plant in Highland Park, Michigan, workers did not move around the factory. The cars moved, but the workers stayed in one place. This system was fast and efficient, and cars became less expensive. Ford sold more than 15 million Model T cars from 1908 to 1927!

Student A

1 Henry Ford was born in (*place*) _____.
2 Ford was born on (*date*) _____.
3 Ford got a job as an engineer in (*year*) _____.
4 In 1896, he invented (*name of invention*) _____.
5 In 1903, Ford started (*name of company*) _____.

Student B

6 Henry Ford became famous because (*reason*) _____.
7 He invented the assembly line in (*year*) _____.
8 The new Ford automobile plant was in (*place*) _____.
9 Ford sold more than (*number of cars*) _____ Model T cars.
10 Ford stopped production of Model T in (*year*) _____.

B Ask your partner questions and complete the sentences for the other paragraph.

B: *Where was Henry Ford born?*
A: *He was born in … Why did Henry Ford become famous?*

C Read both paragraphs more carefully. Check all your sentences for mistakes.

D What other 'great lives' do you know about? Give as much information about their lives as you can.

A Complete the sentences with words from the box.

won	built	invented	explored	wrote	fought	composed	discovered

1 The USA _____ its independence from Great Britain in 1783.
2 Marco Polo _____ China for the first time in 1271.
3 Gustave Eiffel _____ the Eiffel Tower in 1889.
4 The Egyptians _____ cosmetics in 4,000 BC.
5 Anton van Leeuwenhoek _____ bacteria in 1683.
6 Cervantes _____ *Don Quixote* in 1605.
7 Napoleon _____ the Battle of Waterloo in 1815.
8 Georges Bizet _____ the opera *Carmen* in 1875.

B Write a question using a verb from Exercise A. Ask your classmates the question.

A: *Who wrote Hamlet?*
B: *Shakespeare.*

WHAT'S RIGHT?
○ Who invented the radio?
○ Who did invent the radio?

SPEAKING: taking time to think

⚙ Sometimes we need time to think of the answer to a question, or we need to think about the language to use. We use certain words and phrases to give us time to think.

A 🎧**64** Listen to the conversation below. <u>Underline</u> the words and phrases the speakers use to take time to think.

Alison: What were the names of all The Beatles?

Jenny: Uh, I can't remember.

Chris: Let me think. Oh, yeah. Their names were John, Paul, George, and Ringo.

Alison: That's right. And when did George die?

Jenny: Just a second. I'm not sure, but I think he died in 2001.

Chris: Did your parents like The Beatles?

Alison: Well, my dad did, but my mum didn't like them very much.

B 🗣 Work in groups. Answer the quiz together. Take time to think before answering if necessary.

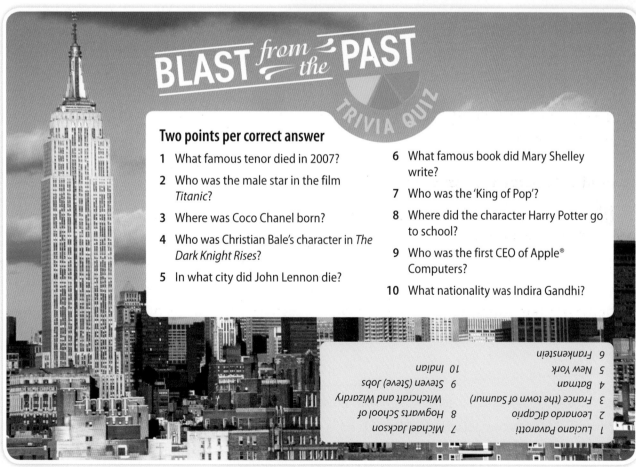

BLAST *from the* PAST
TRIVIA QUIZ

Two points per correct answer

1 What famous tenor died in 2007?

2 Who was the male star in the film *Titanic*?

3 Where was Coco Chanel born?

4 Who was Christian Bale's character in *The Dark Knight Rises*?

5 In what city did John Lennon die?

6 What famous book did Mary Shelley write?

7 Who was the 'King of Pop'?

8 Where did the character Harry Potter go to school?

9 Who was the first CEO of Apple® Computers?

10 What nationality was Indira Gandhi?

1 *Luciano Pavarotti*
2 *Leonardo diCaprio*
3 *France (the town of Saumur)*
4 *Batman*
5 *New York*
6 *Frankenstein*
7 *Michael Jackson*
8 *Hogwarts School of Witchcraft and Wizardry*
9 *Steven (Steve) Jobs*
10 *Indian*

C Check your answers and calculate your score. Which group is the winner?

Great lives **UNIT 11** 133

GRAMMAR: direct and indirect objects

A LANGUAGE IN CONTEXT Read the text below.
How many Nobel Prizes did Marie Curie win?

A young woman, Maria Sklodowska, went from Poland to Paris in 1891 to study at the Sorbonne. Pierre Curie was a lab director at the university. <u>Maria</u> (people now called **her** Marie) met Pierre there and they fell in love. <u>She</u> married **him** in 1895 and they began to work together. In 1898, <u>they</u> discovered <u>polonium</u> and radium, and, in 1903, <u>the Swedish Academy</u> gave **them a Nobel Prize**. They gave **it** to **them** for their discovery of radioactivity. When Pierre Curie died, Marie continued their work. <u>The Academy</u> gave **her a second Nobel Prize** in 1911. They gave **it** to **her** for her work in chemistry.

B ANALYSE: OBJECT PRONOUNS Read the text in Exercise A.

Function Choose the correct option to complete the sentence.

A pronoun replaces a noun / a verb.

> **NOTICE!**
> 1 Look at the words in **bold**. Who or what do they refer to?
> 2 Look at the <u>underlined</u> words. Which are subjects and which are objects?

Form Complete the table.

Subject pronouns	I	you	he	she	it	we	you	they
Object pronouns	me	you	(1) HEM	(2) HER	(3) IT	us	you	(4) THEM

ANALYSE: DIRECT AND INDIRECT OBJECTS Read the text in Exercise A again.

Form Complete the tables with more examples. Then choose the correct option to complete the sentences below.

subject	+ verb	+ person or thing (object)
Maria	met	him there.
They	discovered	polonium.

1 _____

subject	+ verb	+ person (indirect object)	+ thing (direct object)
The Swedish Academy	gave	them	a Nobel Prize.

2 _____

subject	+ verb	+ thing (direct object)	+ preposition	+ person (indirect object)	
They	gave	it	to	them	for their discovery of radioactivity.

3 _____

Note: Verbs like *repeat* and *explain* always follow this structure.

1 When a verb takes two objects, the direct object is usually a thing / a person and the indirect object is usually a thing / a person.
2 Object pronouns always come before / after a verb or a preposition.

C **PRACTISE** Look back through the unit. Answer the questions. Replace the <u>underlined</u> word or words with the correct object pronoun.

1 Who wrote <u>Frankenstein</u>?
Mary Shelley wrote it.

2 Who gave <u>the Curies</u> a Nobel Prize?

3 What company sold <u>Model T cars</u>?

4 When did the Academy give <u>Audrey Hepburn her first Oscar</u>?

5 Who directed <u>Audrey Hepburn</u> in <u>the film *Always*</u>?

6 When did Pierre Curie give <u>Marie a wedding ring</u>?

D **NOW YOU DO IT** Work in groups. Ask and answer these questions.

1 Who is your best friend? When did you meet him/her?
2 What was the last present someone gave you? Did you like it? Why or why not?
3 When was the last time you went out with your friends? Where did you go?

PRONUNCIATION: object pronouns

A))) **65** Listen to the sentences. Are the object pronouns stressed or unstressed?

1 I met David and Lisa at a party.
I met them at a party.

2 I saw my teacher in the park.
I saw him in the park.

B))) **66** Work in pairs. Practise saying the sentences. Then listen and check.

1 My mum loved Fleetwood Mac.
My mum loved them.

2 I gave my brother an MP3 player.
I gave him an MP3 player.

3 Cervantes wrote
Don Quixote in 1605.
Cervantes wrote it in 1605.

WRITING: a short biography

A Read the biographical information about Ray Tomlinson and <u>underline</u> the facts and important information.

Modern inventors: Ray Tomlinson

Ray Tomlinson invented one of the most important things in the modern world – electronic mail, or email. Tomlinson was born in Amsterdam, New York, in 1941. He graduated from the Massachusetts Institute of Technology with a Master's Degree in electrical engineering in 1965. Two years later, he got a job at a technology company. In 1971, Tomlinson wrote a program to send electronic mail between different computers.
Tomlinson used the symbol @ to separate the user from the computer, and we still use that symbol today. We express the symbol as *at*.

B Use the fact file to write a similar biography of Tim Berners–Lee in your notebook.

C Work in groups. Make a list of ten people in history. Read your list to the class and say what each person did.

William Shakespeare wrote many famous plays.

Tim Berners-Lee
Achievement: invented the World Wide Web
Born: London, 8th June, 1955
University: graduated from Oxford University in 1976
First job: at a telecommunications company, as a programmer (1976)
Year he invented the World Wide Web: 1990
Year the Web started on the internet: 1991

LifeSkills

BRAINSTORMING IN A GROUP

- Brainstorm (think of ideas) by yourself.
- Brainstorm with other people. Combine your ideas.
- Choose and develop the best idea or ideas.

A Read the description of the project below and the tips for brainstorming. Then brainstorm ideas by yourself. In your notebook, write as many names in each category of the table below as you can.

> Here is your project …
> You have to choose one person to include in a website about great lives.
> Follow these guidelines.
> • The person should be from your country.
> • The person can be alive or dead.
> • The person should have at least one big achievement in his/her life.

Brainstorming tips (1):
- Think of ideas as fast as you can.
- Do not stop to analyse an idea.
- Do not reject any idea at this time.

Great Lives

Politics	Pop culture	The arts	Sports

B Work in groups. Make a combined list of great lives. What do you notice about the combined list compared with your personal list?

Brainstorming tips (2):
When you brainstorm in a group, ask one person to be the moderator. That person sets a time limit and checks that everyone is contributing ideas. Another person in the group can write down the ideas.

C 🔊 With your group, look at your combined list from Exercise B. Choose one person from the list to write a web entry about.

HOW TO SAY IT 🔊

I think … is good because he/she is/was a very famous …
Do you know a lot about him/her?
What are/were his/her achievements?
I prefer … because …

D 🔊 With your group, complete as much of the word web as you can.

Place

Grew up in

Studied at

Year

CHILDHOOD

Place of birth

FIRST JOB/
ACHIEVEMENT

Name

Date of birth

OTHER
ACHIEVEMENTS

LATER LIFE

Died

Retired

E 🔊 Write a short biography of the person you chose. Choose one person in the group to write the text. The others help with information, grammar, and spelling.

F 🔊 Choose one person in the group to read the biography to your classmates.

REFLECT … How can the skill of brainstorming in a group be useful to you in **Self and Society** and **Work and Career**?

Language wrap-up

1 VOCABULARY

Complete these sentences with words or phrases from the box. (10 points)

had	discovered	wrote	built	composed	retired	grew up	explored	got married	graduated

1 Leo Tolstoy was a Russian novelist. He _____ *War and Peace*.
2 Alexander Fleming was a Scottish bacteriologist. He _____ penicillin.
3 The actor Tommy Lee Jones _____ from Harvard University in 1969. His roommate was Al Gore.
4 Prince William of Great Britain and Catherine Middleton _____ in April 2011 in London.
5 Pelé was one of the world's greatest football players. He finally _____ from the game in 1977.
6 Mozart _____ *Allegro in C* when he was only five years old.
7 Maria Sharapova was born in Russia, but she _____ in the USA.
8 Christopher Columbus _____ the world in the 15th century.
9 The actor and comedian, Charlie Chaplin, _____ eleven children.
10 The emperor Shah Jahan _____ the Taj Mahal in the 17th century.

> **8 – 10 correct:** I can talk about life events and historical events.
> **0 – 7 correct:** Look again at the Vocabulary sections on pages 130 and 132.
> **SCORE:**   /10

2 GRAMMAR

A Rewrite the second sentence of each pair. Replace the <u>underlined</u> words with object pronouns. (6 points)

1 The Olympic® Committee gave medals to the athletes. The athletes thanked <u>the members of the Olympic® Committee</u>.

_____

2 The judges gave the gold medal to Usain Bolt yesterday. He won <u>the gold medal</u> in the 100m.

_____

3 I know that you and John like this magazine. I saved <u>this magazine</u> for <u>you and John</u>.

_____

4 I'm interested in the life of Queen Elizabeth the First. I wrote a short biography about <u>Queen Elizabeth the First</u>.

_____

5 Oh, this article is about John Lennon! I like to read about <u>John Lennon</u>.

_____

B Rewrite the sentences using a *when* clause. Use a comma if necessary. (4 points)

1 My girlfriend sent me a postcard from Paris. I was very happy.
I _____.
2 Joanna and Marcus invited us over for dinner. We were really surprised.
We _____.
3 The teacher gave George an A for his history exam. He was really excited.
When _____.
4 Anna's husband gave her a nice gift. She hugged him.
When _____.

> **8 – 10 correct:** I can use the past simple with *when* clauses. I can use object pronouns.
> **0 – 7 correct:** Look again at the Grammar sections on pages 131 and 134.
> **SCORE:**   /10

A Tick the types of information that you think are necessary in a short biography.

☐ the person's middle name
☐ place of birth
☐ date of birth
☐ favourite activities as a child
☐ the names of brothers and sisters
☐ where the person studied
☐ what he/she got a degree in
☐ his/her favourite subjects
☐ major achievements
☐ date of death if the person is dead

B Read the text. Then number the facts in the order that they appear in the text.

_____ Date of birth
_____ Date of death
_____ Where he studied
_____ Major achievement
_____ Place of birth
_____ His first job

Famous entrepreneurs
Steven Jobs

Steven Jobs was born on 24th February, 1955. He was born in Wisconsin, but he grew up in California. Jobs was very intelligent, but he didn't like school. When he finished high school, he entered Reed College in Oregon, but he stayed in the university for only six months. In 1974, Jobs got a job with Atari® as a video game designer. Then in 1976, he and his friend Steve Wozniak started Apple® Computers in Jobs's family garage. The little company became a multi-billion-dollar corporation. This great entrepreneur died of cancer on 5th October, 2011.

C Do research on a famous person you are interested in. Make notes on the texts you read. Decide which information to include in a very short biographical text. Number the information in the order you want to include it.

D Write a short biography of the person. Refer to your notes, but write the biography in your own words. Include at least one sentence with a *when* clause.

HOW ARE YOU DOING?

Look back at your writing and tick the statements that are true.
○ The facts in the biography are in a logical order.
○ All of the information in the biography is relevant and necessary.
○ The verbs are in the correct tense.
○ There is at least one sentence with a *when* clause.

Now ask your partner to look at your writing and tick.

Did you find out important facts about the person's life? Were the facts in a logical order?

● Well done!   ● Nearly!   ● Think again!

UNIT 12 IN THE NEAR FUTURE

IN THIS UNIT YOU

- ⚙ learn language to talk about plans, intentions, and resolutions
- ⚙ listen to people talking about holiday plans
- ⚙ write about plans for making changes in your life
- ⚙ talk about plans and holiday arrangements
- ⚙ read about New Year's resolutions
- ⚙ create a plan for improving your English
- ▶ watch a video about future plans

LISTENING
understanding the main idea
What key words can help you identify the main idea in a conversation about a holiday?

WRITING
sequencing and connecting ideas
What different words can we use to connect more than one idea? What ideas do we connect in this unit?

LIFE SKILLS

STUDY & LEARNING

analysing strengths and weaknesses
When we talk about 'strengths' and 'weaknesses', what do we mean? Why is it important to understand your strengths and weaknesses?

A How much do you plan your life? Tick (✓) the statement that best describes you.

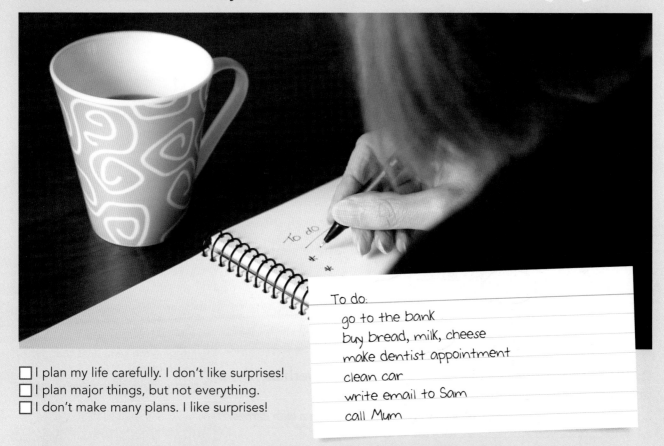

To do:
go to the bank
buy bread, milk, cheese
make dentist appointment
clean car
write email to Sam
call Mum

☐ I plan my life carefully. I don't like surprises!
☐ I plan major things, but not everything.
☐ I don't make many plans. I like surprises!

B Compare your answer in Exercise A with your classmates. How many people chose each statement? Say what types of things you like to plan and what you don't like to plan.

A: *So, how do you feel about making plans?*
B: *Well, planning makes me feel organised so I plan everything carefully. I don't like surprises! What about you?*
A: *I'm the same.*

Hmm ... what do I want to do today?

HOW TO SAY IT

Talking about yourself

I like to plan everything / things I have to do for work or school / my weekend activities.

Planning makes me feel organised/happy/calm.

I make plans, but I never follow them!

I'm the same.

I'm not like that at all.

A »🎧 **67** **LANGUAGE IN CONTEXT** Listen to the conversation below. Choose the time Victor is free to meet his friend.

Victor: Hello?

Amy: Hi, Victor. It's Amy.

Victor: Oh, hi, Amy.

Amy: Do you have any plans for this evening?

Victor: I'm staying at home. I have to study.

Amy: Oh, OK. That's a shame! What about tomorrow afternoon?

Victor: Let's see … No, I'm not doing anything. Shall we have lunch together? Let's go to Greens. I love that place.

Amy: OK. Hey, I'm having a party on Friday. Do you want to come?

Victor: Oh, I can't! I'm going on holiday on Friday.

Amy: OK, never mind. Anyway, see you tomorrow afternoon.

Victor: Yeah, sure. See you tomorrow!

Victor is free …

a) this evening.   b) tomorrow afternoon.   c) Friday evening.

B ANALYSE Read the conversation in Exercise A again.

Function Choose the correct option to complete the sentences.

1 The conversation is about the present / the future.

2 Victor's plans are definite / possible but not definite.

Form Choose the correct option to complete the sentence.

3 Victor uses the present simple / present continuous to talk about his plans.

NOTICE!

Is the conversation about activities the people are doing at the moment or activities in the future?

<u>Underline</u> the sentences that refer to plans.

C PRACTISE Complete the sentences with the verb in brackets in the correct form.

1 I can't see you tomorrow. I _____ (go) to the cinema with James.

2 What _____ you _____ (do) tomorrow night?

3 We _____ (visit) my grandparents this weekend.

4 Lorena and Ali _____ (come) for dinner on Friday.

5 I _____ (not do) anything tomorrow. Do you want to have lunch?

6 _____ Simon _____ (work) next week?

WHAT'S RIGHT?

◯ I'm go out tonight.

◯ I'm going out tonight.

◯ I go out tonight.

D 🔊 **NOW YOU DO IT** Tick (✓) or complete the activities you are definitely planning for the weekend. Then discuss your plans in pairs.

☐ working
☐ studying
☐ going to the cinema
☐ going shopping
☐ going out
☐ visiting family
☐ going swimming
☐ other: _____

A: *What are you doing this weekend?*

B: *Well, on Saturday I'm not working. I'm going to the cinema with some friends, and then we're going dancing. On Sunday …*

PRONUNCIATION: verbs ending with -y +ing

A 🔊 **68** Listen to these words. Write 2 or 3 next to each word, according to the number of syllables you hear.

playing _____   marrying _____   paying _____
worrying _____   staying _____   studying _____

B 🔊 Practise saying the words. Listen, check and practise again.

C 🔊 🔊 **69** Work in pairs. Practise saying these sentences. Listen and check.

1 I'm playing in the football final on Saturday.
2 I'm staying at home and studying on Sunday.
3 My sister is marrying her fiancé next Saturday.

LISTENING: understanding the main idea page 121 ⚙

A 🔊 **70** Listen to the conversation. In your notebook, write down any key words you hear that are repeated.

B 🔊 **70** Look at your list of key words and answer the questions. Then listen again to check.

1 What is the main topic of the conversation?
   a) The history of Thailand   b) Rick's favourite beaches   c) Charlie's holiday plans
2 What is Charlie's main interest?
   a) beaches   b) Buddhist temples   c) Greek architecture
3 Does Rick think Charlie's holiday sounds exciting? Why or why not?

C 🔊 **70** Listen to the conversation again. Answer the questions.

1 What is Charlie doing in Thailand? _____
2 Is Charlie visiting many beaches in Thailand? _____
3 Where is Rick going on holiday? _____

D 🔊 What are your favourite holiday destinations in your own country?

A: *My favourite place for a holiday is … because I'm interested in history.*
B: *Really? I prefer … because I love being outside.*

A [icon] [icon] **71** Listen and repeat the phrases. Say which activities in the photos you do.

Activities with *go* + gerund

GO

swimming

running

horse riding

walking

dancing

cycling

I sometimes go running. I never go swimming.

B [icon] Work in groups. Talk about which of the things in Exercise A you are doing in the near future.

A: *I'm going swimming tomorrow.*
B: *Where?*
A: *At my gym.*
C: *How often do you go swimming?*
A: *Three times a week.*

shopping

A [icon] **72** **LANGUAGE IN CONTEXT** Listen to the conversation below. Why is Stefan unhappy?

Stefan: Oh, no! Look at my marks! That's it. I'm going to improve my English!

Marie: How? What are you going to do?

Stefan: Well, first, I'm going to study every day.

Marie: Oh, sure!

Stefan: I am! And I'm going to get a summer job in Ireland.

Marie: Oh, yeah? And are you going to get an Irish girlfriend, too …?

Stefan: Yes, I am! So I'm not going to speak Dutch at all. Only English.

Marie: They sound like good ideas. Don't worry about it now, anyway. I'm going dancing with some friends tonight. Do you want to come?

Stefan: Sure, that sounds fun. What time are you going?

Marie: Well, we're going to a Greek restaurant for dinner first, so we're meeting at Lenny's at 7.30.

Stefan: OK, great. Listen, I have to go. I'm going swimming with Julio.

Marie: OK, have fun.

Stefan: Thanks. See you at Lenny's!

NOTICE!

Look at the underlined phrases. In which sentence can you replace 'am/are going' with 'plan'?

B ANALYSE Read the conversation in Exercise A again.

Function Choose the correct option to complete the sentences.
1 We use *going to* / *the present continuous* to talk about definite plans and arrangements.
2 We use *going to* / *the present continuous* to talk about less definite plans and intentions.

Form Choose the correct option to complete the sentence. Then complete the table.
With *going to*, we use the verb in *the base form* / *the -ing form*.

be + going to + verb	
Affirmative statements	(1) I _____ improve my English.
Negative statements	(2) I _____ speak Dutch.
Questions and answers	(3) _____ you _____ get an Irish girlfriend? (4) Yes, _____ . / No, I'm not.
	(5) What _____ you _____ do to improve your English?

C PRACTISE Look at the pictures. Write about what each person is going to do.

1 He going to listen music

2 They going to

3 He wanted make a cake, cook someth. new.

4 She is leaving a library. She going to read the book.

5 They are going to buy

6 going to lessons.

D 🔊 NOW YOU DO IT Work in groups. Tell your group about some of your intentions.

A: I'm going to study more.
B: And I'm going to visit my grandparents more often.
C: Well, I'm going to travel to a foreign country next year.

WHAT'S RIGHT?
◯ He goes to call me tonight.
◯ He's going to call me tonight.
◯ He calls me tonight.

SPEAKING: talking about plans

A Work in pairs. Read the conversation about people's plans. Then answer the questions below.

Jenny: What are you guys going to do over the summer?

Michael: I'm not going to have a lot of free time this summer because I'm volunteering at an animal shelter. I'm starting in two weeks. I love animals, and I'm probably going to adopt a dog from the shelter. I'm really excited!

Georgia: My cousin is arriving from Australia next week, and she's staying for a month. I'm excited because I'm going to meet her in person for the first time! It's going to be fun.

Jenny: I love cycling, so I'm going to join the Edinburgh Cycling Club. They're having a 50-mile ride on 1st June, from Edinburgh to Glasgow, and I'm going to do that. I need to get fit for it!

1 What is Michael probably going to do?
2 Why is Georgia excited?
3 Why does Jenny need to get fit?

B Make some notes about what you are going to do on your next holiday.

C Work in small groups. Tell your group about your holiday plans.

I have great plans for the holidays. I'm going to … I'm probably … Then I'm going to … in the Lake District.

VOCABULARY: intentions

A Look at the pictures and tick (✓) the good habits.

exercise | set goals | study | eat fast food | worry | think positively

B In your notebook, write six sentences that are true for you using phrases from Exercise A.

I'm going to start exercising …
I'm going to stop …
I want to start/stop …

C Work in pairs. Read the sentences you wrote in Exercise B and make appropriate responses to your partner's sentences.

A: *I'm going to stop eating fast food.*
B: *Me, too! And I want to start exercising.*
A: *Good idea.*

WRITING: sequencing and connecting ideas page 122

Remember that you can use these sequencing words to put your ideas in order:
first, then, next, after that, finally.

A Tick (✓) four things that you want to change in your life.

- ☐ exercise
- ☐ stop eating fast food
- ☐ study more
- ☐ organise my time
- ☐ spend more time with friends
- ☐ stop smoking
- ☐ lose weight
- ☐ change my appearance
- ☐ learn to _____

B Write the four things in the order that you're going to do them.

C Write about the changes you are going to make. Remember to use sequencing words.

I'm going to make some changes … . First, I'm going to … . Then, I'm going to …

A Read the blog and answer the questions.

1 Why do people celebrate the end of one year and the beginning of another year?
2 Why don't all countries celebrate New Year on 31ˢᵗ December?
3 What do New Year's celebrations have in common?

New Year's resolutions
around the world

People all over the world celebrate the beginning of a new year as a symbol for change and new beginnings. Different cultures celebrate New Year at different times, depending on their traditional calendar. In most Western countries, the last day of the year (New Year's Eve) is 31ˢᵗ December, but the dates of Chinese New Year and Islamic New Year are different every year. However, most New Year's celebrations have one thing in common. In many countries, people make New Year's resolutions about changes they are going to make in their lives and things they are going to do in the coming year. Of course, most of us forget about our New Year's resolutions very soon after New Year and go back to our old bad habits!

We want to know if New Year's resolutions are similar in different cultures and countries. We're asking you to leave a comment and tell us some of your resolutions. So tell us, what are your New Year's resolutions this year?

B Read the comments section and choose T (true) or F (false).

1 Cathy wants to eat less fast food.	T / F
2 Dhom wants to see more of his family.	T / F
3 Abdul is going to work less.	T / F
4 This is the first time Sigi has tried to stop smoking.	T / F
5 Alicia is happy with her weight.	T / F
6 Leo wants to do more exercise.	T / F

C Add a comment to the blog. Write the resolutions that you are going to make on the next New Year's Day.

D Work in groups. Read all your comments in your group. One person writes the comments down. Then 'post' your comments on the wall.

E Walk around and read all of the comments. Then discuss these questions as a class.

- Are many of the resolutions similar to each other?
- Are they also similar to the resolutions in the blog in Exercise A?
- What are the most common resolutions?
- Why do you think New Year's resolutions tend to be similar?

Friday, 09.14
Cathy, Australia:
I want to be healthier. I'm going to stop eating fast food. Definitely.

Friday, 12.36
Dhom, Thailand:
I'm very busy with my job, but I'm going to try to spend more time with my family.

Friday, 14.40
Abdul, Algeria:
I'm going to work harder because I hope to get a promotion this year.

Friday, 19.21
Sigi, Germany:
I'm finally going to stop smoking. My family is going to help me. This time I'm not going to give up!

Friday, 23.57
Alicia, Colombia:
I'm going to lose weight. I'm going to join a gym and a walking club.

Saturday 02.46
Leo, Spain:
I'm going to start exercising. That's a common resolution, but I'm really going to do it!

LifeSkills

ANALYSING STRENGTHS AND WEAKNESSES

- Determine the areas you want to evaluate yourself in.
- Evaluate your strengths and weaknesses.
- Identify ways to improve your weaknesses.
- Set realistic goals.

A You are going to evaluate your abilities in English. Look at the areas of English in the table below and think of two more to complete the list.

B Evaluate your abilities in these areas of English. What things do you find easy and what do you find difficult? Tick the appropriate column in the table. Then look at the table as a whole. Which areas are strengths for you? Which are weaknesses?

	Very strong	Strong	Average	Weak	Very weak
Listening					
Speaking					
Reading					
Grammar					
Pronunciation					

C Complete the table below to help you identify activities to improve your English.

- Tick (✓) Column 1 for activities that are easy to do in your town, city or country.
- Tick (✓) Column 2 for activities that you enjoy.
- In Column 3, write the letter of the skill that the activity helps you improve.
  Write L (listening), S (speaking), R (reading), W (writing), G (grammar), V (vocabulary), P (pronunciation).
- Many of the activities give practice in several areas, so Column 3 can have more than one answer.

Things that can help your English	Easy to do in your area?	Enjoyable?	Skill(s) it improves
Reading magazines/articles in English			
Watching TV/DVDs without subtitles			
Talking to people from other countries			
Forming a conversation group			
Travelling to other English-speaking countries			
Listening to songs / the radio in English			
Chatting online to international friends			
Writing emails in English			

D Work in groups. Compare your answers in Exercise B. If necessary, change your answers.

E Look back at your evaluation in Exercise B. Use the ideas for activities in Exercise C as well as your own ideas to make an action plan for improving the weak areas of your English.

Goals for improving my English

Areas I want to improve	Things I'm going to do	How often
Listening	Watch DVDs without subtitles	Once a week

F Work in groups. Explain your plan from Exercise E. Your group can ask questions or make suggestions.

I want to improve my listening and my speaking.
I'm going to watch DVDs without subtitles at least once a week.
I'm also going to …

When you make a plan, don't try to plan too much. It's better to start with a few goals and then increase your goals little by little.

? **REFLECT …** How can the skill of analysing strengths and weaknesses be useful to you in **Self and Society** and **Work and Career**?

Language wrap-up

A Complete the sentences with words from the box. (5 points)

| running | walking | cycling | dancing | swimming |

1. I really should go _____ more. I never use my bicycle.
2. I want to go _____ again. There's an amazing pool near my flat.
3. I'm going _____ next week. I want to learn samba.
4. I should go _____ in the park. I just need to buy some trainers.
5. I want to go _____ more. There are a lot of nice places to explore near here.

B Complete the sentences with *start* or *stop* and words/phrases from the box. (5 points)

| eating fast food | going out | exercising | studying | worrying |

1. I'm going to _____ more. I want to improve my marks.
2. I'm going to _____. All these burgers and chips are not good for me.
3. I'm going to _____ every week. There's a really good gym near my house.
4. I'm going to _____ about the future so much. Life is too short.
5. I really want to _____ with my friends more. I stay at home too often.

8 – 10 correct: I can use expressions with *go, start,* and *stop* to talk about intentions.

0 – 7 correct: Look again at the Vocabulary sections on pages 144 and 146.

SCORE: /10

GRAMMAR

A Use Max's diary to complete the sentences using the present continuous. (5 points)

1. Max _____ lunch with Mr Austin at 12.30pm.
2. He and Mr Austin _____ the office at 2pm.
3. Max _____ in his office all afternoon.
4. He _____ Emma for dinner at 7.30pm.
5. Max and Emma _____ dinner at Le Bistro.

FRIDAY APRIL 4

12.30 Have lunch Mr Austin

2.00 visit office with Mr A.

3.00–6.00 work in office

7.30 meet Emma ♡♡

8.30 have dinner at Le Bistro

B Complete the conversation between Max and Jim with *going to* and the verb in brackets. (5 points)

Jim: Hey, I hear you're going to the beach next week. What (1) _____ you _____ (do) while you're there?

Max: Well, I (2) _____ (relax). I (3) _____ (not think) about work for a week. I (4) _____ (read) a good book, play tennis, and lie on the beach. Emma (5) _____ (take) surfing lessons. She doesn't like too much relaxation.

8 – 10 correct: I can use the present continuous to talk about plans and arrangements and *going to* to talk about plans and intentions.

0 – 7 correct: Look again at the Grammar sections on pages 142 and 144.

SCORE: /10

SPEAKING WORKSHOP

A Read the conversation. In your opinion, is Paul doing well or badly at keeping his promise?

Martin: So did you make any New Year's resolutions?

Paul: No, but last month I made a promise to my family. My promise was that I'm going to spend less time using social media and more time doing things with them. I decided to do it because I want to have a better relationship with my family, especially my parents.

Martin: And how's it going?

Paul: Well, now I always do something with my brother and sister at the weekend. That's going really well, but I'm not sure about my relationship with my parents. They think all social media are dangerous, but I don't want to stop using them completely! I'm going to ask them to read some of my posts on Facebook and Twitter. Maybe I can convince them that social media can be useful!

B Find and <u>underline</u> the following things in the conversation in Exercise A.

- Paul's resolution
- Paul's reason for his resolution
- What Paul is doing now to keep his resolution
- What Paul is going to do in the future

C Work in pairs. Think of a promise or resolution that you made last New Year or in the recent past. Tell your partner about your resolution.

Things to include:
- what you want to do (your resolution)
- a reason for your resolution
- an explanation of what you are doing to keep your resolution
- an explanation of what you are going to do in the future to keep your resolution

D Now work with a different partner. Tell him or her about your resolution. Include things from the list in Exercise C.

HOW ARE YOU DOING?

Think about your speaking. Do you feel confident:
○ using *going to* to talk about resolutions?
○ explaining your resolutions and why you want to do them?
○ explaining what you are doing to keep your resolutions?

How do you feel about your speaking generally?

●   ○   ●

Very confident!   Not sure…   Need to practise

Grammar Reference

BE – STATEMENTS AND YES/NO QUESTIONS

Form

Affirmative			Negative	
I am (I'm)			I am not (I'm not)	
You are (You're)			You are not (You aren't / You're not)	
He/She/It is (He's/She's/It's)	from New York.		He is not (He isn't / He's not)	from Tokyo.
We are (We're)			We are not (We aren't / We're not)	
They are (They're)			They are not (They aren't / They're not)	

Yes/No questions		Short answers
Are you		Yes, I am. / No, I'm not.
Is he/she/it	in England?	Yes, he/she/it is. / No, he/she/it isn't.
Are we		Yes, we are. / No, we're not.
Are they		Yes, they are. / No, they aren't.

Function

We use the verb **be** to talk about people and things and facts about them, such as age and name. We use *yes/no* questions when we want to know if something is true or false.

1 Complete the sentences with the words from the box.

am   is   are   not   isn't   aren't

1 My name _____ Alice Reed.
2 You _____ from my home town! Wow!
3 I'm _____ from Mexico. I'm from Brazil.
4 Ella and Tom _____ here. They're at the park.
5 Daniel _____ my brother. He's my cousin.
6 I _____ 19 years old.
7 _____ he an English student?
8 _____ they from Germany?

2 Match 1–5 with a–e to complete the sentences.

1 Sam, you
2 Hello. I
3 My address
4 John
5 Pierre and I

a) aren't from the USA, but from Canada.
b) is 221 Bridge Street.
c) are funny!
d) isn't in school today.
e) am on your course at university.

BE – Wh- QUESTIONS

Form

What	is your name?	Who	are you?
	is your address?		is Luis Tosar?
Where	are you from?	When	is your birthday?
	is Marta?	How old	are you?

Function

We use information questions when the answer we want is a thing, a person, a place, a time, etc.

1 Choose the correct option.

1 What is your name / your name is?
2 Where / When are you from?
3 How old they are / are they?
4 When / How is your birthday?
5 Who / What is Peter?
6 What is your number / your number is?

2 Write questions using the prompts.

1 (your address) "_____?"
   "It's 44 Westminster Street."
2 (Richard and Mark) "_____?"
   "They're 20 years old."
3 (your birthday) "_____?"
   "It's 12ᵗʰ February."
4 (your brother) "_____?"
   "Steven, the man with the brown hair."
5 (our class) "_____?"
   "It's in Room 6A."

UNIT 2

ARTICLES

Form

zero (no) article		I like cats.
indefinite article	a/an	I'm a doctor. I'm an actor.
definite article	the	The sky is blue.

We use **an** instead of **a** before singular nouns that begin with a vowel, e.g. *an artist*.

Function

We use the indefinite article with jobs and professions.	I'm a singer.
We use the indefinite article to talk about non-specific singular nouns.	I want to eat an apple. (any apple, not a particular one) She's a beautiful girl. (Here's an example of a beautiful girl)
We don't use an article with plural nouns when we want to make a general reference.	I like apples. (apples in general, not particular apples)
We use the indefinite article with a singular noun when we use it for the first time. We use the definite article after that.	I see a man. The man is tall and handsome.
We also use the definite article with specific nouns and things there is only one of: the sun, the sky, the government, etc.	You can eat the apples on the table. (particular apples, not any apples).

1 Complete the sentences with *a, an, the* or – (no article).

1 I want to be _____ teacher and work in _____ school.
2 My dad's in _____ navy. It's _____ good job.
3 I love _____ video games! _____ new game for the Xbox is great!
4 Is your sister _____ architect? Or is she _____ engineer?
5 Justin's _____ writer. He has _____ office at home.

2 Complete the sentences with the correct option.

1 I love working for _____ government.
   a) the   b) a   c) (no article)

2 Is _____ good salary important to you?
   a) a   b) an   c) (no article)

3 My brother wants to be _____ designer.
   a) the   b) a   c) (no article)

4 The manager has _____ office next to me.
   a) a   b) the   c) (no article)

5 _____ English teachers help students to learn.
   a) The   b) An   c) (no article)

POSSESSION: *have got*

Form

	Affirmative	Negative	Questions	Short answers
I/you/we/they	have got / 've got	haven't got	Have I/you/we/they got brown hair?	Yes, I/you/we/they have. No, I/you/we/they haven't.
he/she/it	has got / 's got	hasn't got	Has he/she/it got a bag?	Yes, he/she/it has. No, he/she/it hasn't.

Function

We often use the expression **have got** instead of **have** to talk about what people own or possess.
I've got two brothers. (= I have two brothers.)
He's got brown eyes. (= He has brown eyes.)

POSSESSION: apostrophe

Form

Singular nouns / Irregular plural nouns	Regular plural nouns
noun + 's + noun	noun + ' + noun
e.g. Jodie's hair / the children's toys	e.g. sisters' jobs

Function

We use **'s** and **'** to show that someone has something.
Jodie's hair = the hair of Jodie (the hair Jodie has)
my sisters' jobs = the jobs of my sisters (the jobs my sisters have)

WHOSE

Form

whose + noun + verb / *whose* + verb + noun
e.g. *Whose book is this? / Whose is this book?*

Function

We use **whose** to ask who something belongs to.
Whose car is this? / Whose is this car? = Who does this car belong to?

POSSESSIVE PRONOUNS

Form

I	you	he	she	we	you	they
mine	yours	his	hers	ours	yours	theirs

Function

We use pronouns when we don't want to repeat a noun or a noun phrase. Possessive pronouns replace noun phrases. We use them to say who things belong to.

Whose is this pen? It's Kate's pen. (= The pen belongs to Kate.) *It's hers.*
Whose shoes are these? They're my shoes. (= The shoes belong to me.) *They're mine.*

*Note: There is no possessive pronoun for *it*.

1 Choose the correct option.

1 Dad hasn't / haven't got black hair.
2 Is this Laura's / Lauras' book or not?
3 Ed has / have got a great job.
4 Here's the Smiths' / Smith's address. Contact me there.
5 I hasn't / haven't got Jason's mobile number.
6 Where is your parents' / parent's house?

2 Put the words in the correct order to form questions. Then complete the sentences with a possessive pronoun.

1 books / are / whose / the / ? (Linda and Paul)

_____

They're _____.

2 pen / whose / is / the / ? (Matt)

_____

It's _____.

3 they / video / are / Amy's / games / ? (Me and Sara)

_____

No, they're _____.

4 he / brother / is / Paul's / ? (Me)

_____

No, he's _____.

5 is / whose / the / jacket / ? (Anna)

_____

It's _____.

UNIT 3

PRESENT SIMPLE – STATEMENTS AND *YES/NO* QUESTIONS

Form

Affirmative/Negative

I/You/We/They	like / don't like	music.
He/She/It	buys / doesn't buy	

Yes/No questions

Do I/you/we/they	like music?
Does he/she/it	

Short answers

Yes,	I/you/we/they	do.
No,		don't.
Yes,	he/she/it	does.
No,		doesn't.

Spelling rules for 3rd person singular (he/she/it):
- most verbs, add -s: e.g. *like – likes   say – says   meet – meets*
- verbs that end in consonant + y, take off the -y and add -ies: e.g. *study – studies   try – tries*
- verbs that end in -s, -z, -ch, -sh, -x, -o, add -es: e.g. *watch – watches   relax – relaxes*
                                                         do – does   go – goes

Irregular verbs: *have – has*

Function

We use the present simple to talk about and describe:
- facts that are generally true;
- feelings and states;
- routines and habits.

---

1 Underline the mistake in each sentence. Then correct it.

1 My brother like music and he downloads lots of songs. _____
2 Do Sarah have any interesting hobbies? _____
3 I love this song, but my girlfriend don't like it at all! _____
4 I doesn't buy many CDs, but I buy a lot of MP3s. _____
5 This sounds like a great song! Does you like it? _____
6 Does Simon plays the piano? Yes, he does. _____

2 Complete the text with the correct form of the verb.

What's Olivia's daily routine? Well, she usually (1) _____ (wake up) at seven. She (2) _____ (have) a shower and then breakfast. She (3) _____ (leave) the house to catch the train to the shop where she (4) _____ (work). The shop (5) _____ (open) at nine. They (6) _____ (not have) many customers before 9.30 most days. The other workers and Olivia (7) _____ (serve) customers all day until 5pm. (8) _____ she _____ (like) her job? Yes, she does. It (9) _____ (not pay) her a lot of money, but she (10) _____ (not have) any worries either!

PRESENT SIMPLE – INFORMATION QUESTIONS

Form

Question word	Auxiliary	Subject	Verb
What/Where/When/ Why/Who	do	I/you/we/they	watch/do/etc ...?
	does	he/she/it	

Function

We use question words to ask questions and find out information about things (**what**), people (**who**), places (**where**), times (**when**) and reasons (**why**).

1 Tick (✓) the correct sentences. If a sentence has a mistake, <u>underline</u> the mistake and write the correct form.

1 Who do you go to the cinema with? _____
2 Why does Richard stays in that job? _____
3 Where do you go on holiday? _____
4 When do Alex and his colleagues start work? _____
5 What does you do for a living? _____

2 Write questions using the prompts.

1 (when / Will / play golf) "_____?"
   "Every Saturday morning, I think."
2 (where / you / work?) "_____?"
   "Me? In the big building on Revolution Road."
3 (why / Rafael and Mike / arrive late every day) "_____?"
   "Because the bus is always late!"
4 (who / Leon / look like) "_____?"
   "He looks just like his dad!"
5 (what / I / need for the meeting) "_____?"
   "Just bring your notebook."

UNIT 4

ADVERBS OF FREQUENCY AND ADVERBIAL PHRASES

Function

We use adverbs of frequency to describe how often something happens. Different adverbs of frequency describe different levels of frequency:

0% ⟵———————————————⟶ 100%

never   rarely   sometimes   often   usually   always

We can also use adverbial phrases such as *once a month*, *twice a week*, etc, to describe how often something happens.

once a month = one time in a month
twice a year = two times in a year

Form

Adverbs of frequency normally come before the verb: subject + adverb + verb
I **never** forget people's names.
However, they always come after the verb *be*: subject + *be* + adverb
I am **rarely** late for work.

Adverbial phrases can come at the beginning or at the end of a clause:
Once a week, I go out with friends. I go out with friends once a week.
*Note: If the adverbial phrase comes at the beginning of the clause, use a comma.

1 Complete each sentence using the verb and frequency adverb.

1 Peter _____ polite and listens to everyone's opinion. (be / always)

2 I _____ I need to find a new hobby. (think / often)

3 _____ you _____ the bus home after school? (catch / always)

4 You _____ too old to start a new hobby! (be / never)

5 They _____ good quiz shows on TV. (show / rarely)

6 I _____ too busy to go to the gym. (be / sometimes)

2 Complete the sentences with the words from the box.

always	often	once	rarely	week

1 I see Jake twice a _____ for coffee.

2 Tim _____ beats me at chess. I never win!

3 It _____ rains here in the winter – almost every week!

4 I go on holiday _____ a year, in the summer.

5 She _____ sends me emails now – maybe one a month.

CLAUSES WITH *UNTIL*, *BEFORE*, *AFTER*

Form

We use **until**, **before**, and **after** to connect two clauses together. The clauses can come in either order:

I brush my teeth. I have a shower.   *I brush my teeth before I have a shower.*
                                      Before I have a shower, I brush my teeth.

*Note: Use a comma if the clause with *until*, *before*, or *after* comes first.

Function

We use **before** and **after** to talk about the order of events.
We use **before** with the second event: *I always touch the grass (1)* **before** *I start to play. (2)*
We use **after** with the first event: **After** *I do that, (1) I always play well. (2)*
We use **until** to talk about the duration of events.
We use **until** to talk about an event that continues up to another event or a specific time:
I stay in the dressing room **until** *the other players leave.*

1 Choose the correct meaning of each sentence.

1 I always have a shower before I go swimming.
   a) I go swimming first.   b) I have a shower first.

2 I study in the morning until my class starts.
   a) I study first.   b) My class starts first.

3 The bus usually comes after the train leaves.
   a) The bus comes first.   b) The train leaves first.

4 Until his dad comes home from work, Harry plays video games.
   a) Harry plays video games first. b) Harry's dad comes home first.

5 After I finish my job at the restaurant, I work at the garage.
   a) I work at the restaurant first. b) I work at the garage first.

6 Before she cooks, Jen always washes her hands.
   a) She cooks first.   b) She washes her hands first.

2 Rewrite as one sentence using the word given.

1 I finish studying. Then, I call my friends. (before)
   _____

2 Olivia and Sara play tennis. Then, they get tired and stop. (until)
   _____

3 I cook. Then, my wife does the washing up. (after)
   _____

4 The children play outside. Then, it's time to eat. (until)
   _____

5 I finish work. Then, I go bowling with my friends. (after)
   _____

6 I go to the gym. Then, I go to work. (before)
   _____

THERE IS / THERE ARE WITH SOME, ANY, SEVERAL, A LOT OF, MANY

Form

	Singular	Plural
Affirmative	There is a new shopping centre in my town.	There are **some / several / many / a lot of** festivals at this time of year.
Negative	There isn't a music festival this year.	There aren't **any / many / a lot of** concerts.
Questions	Is there a good Chinese restaurant near here?	Are there **any / many / a lot of** museums in your city?

*Note: We can also use the contraction *there's* instead of *there is*.

Function
We use **there is / there are** to say that something exists.
We use **some, any, several, a lot of**, and **many** to talk about general quantities.

1 Complete the sentences with correct forms of *there is / there are*.

1 _____ any interesting events this month?
2 _____ a film festival in my city every year. It's really good.
3 _____ any good films on right now.
4 _____ many nice shops in my area, so we usually go to the city centre to shop.
5 _____ a lot of people at the festival?
6 _____ a science museum in my city, but there is a planetarium.

2 Choose the correct option.

1 There aren't several / many good films this time of year.
2 There are several / any good restaurants near here.
3 I go to a lot of / any concerts.
4 There aren't a lot of festivals in this area, but there are many / some festivals.
5 There aren't any / some good photos of the festival on this website.

THE IMPERATIVE

Function
We use the imperative to give instructions or directions.

Form

Affirmative	Negative
base form	*don't* + base form
Turn right on Park Street.	**Don't worry**.
Please **write** your name.	Please **don't be** late!

1 Correct the mistakes with the imperatives.

1 No get lost! _____
2 Please to sit down. _____
3 Turn you left at the traffic lights. _____
4 Doesn't worry about the exam. _____
5 Please talk not during the film. _____

2 Look at the signs and pictures. Complete the sentences with the verbs from the box. Use the correct form.

walk	turn	be	make	watch	run

1 _____ left.
2 Please _____ quiet.
3 _____ near the pool.

4 _____ straight ahead.
5 Please _____ TV right now.
6 _____ a U-turn.

PRESENT CONTINUOUS

Function

We use the present continuous with situations or events that are happening right at this moment or around now.

Form

Subject + *be* + present participle (verb + *-ing*)

Affirmative/Negative

I	am / am not	
He/She/It	is / is not	working.
You/We/They	are / are not	

Yes/No questions		
Am	I	
Is	he/she/it	working?
Are	you/we/they	

Short answers		
Yes, I am.	No, I'm not.
Yes, he/she/it is.	No, he/she/it isn't.
Yes, you/we/they are.	No, you/we/they aren't.

Information questions

Where	is	he/she/it	working?
What	are	you/they	doing?
Why	are	you/they	leaving?
When	is	he/she/it	coming?
Who	are	we	meeting?

Spelling rules for present participles:
* When the verb ends in -e, drop the -e and add -ing, e.g. *take – taking*.
* When the verb has one syllable and ends in consonant-vowel-consonant, double the final consonant and add -ing, e.g. *plan – planning*.

1 Write the present participles for these verbs.

1 run _____
2 study _____
3 give _____
4 wait _____
5 swim _____

6 have _____
7 worry _____
8 see _____
9 sit _____
10 visit _____

2 Complete the questions and answers. Use the verbs in brackets.

1 _____ Bill and Lisa _____ to the party? (*come*)
Yes, _____ .
2 Where _____ Malcolm _____? (*study*)
He _____ in the library.
3 _____ Carol _____ at a design studio? (*work*)
No, she _____ . She _____ at an art gallery.
4 _____ you _____ anyone at the moment? (*date*)
No, _____ .
5 Who _____ Peter _____ to on the phone? (*talk*)
He _____ to his sister.

PRESENT CONTINUOUS VS PRESENT SIMPLE

Function
We use the present simple to talk about things that are generally true or are permanent situations. We use the present continuous to talk about things that are happening right now or around now.

*Note: We don't use the present continuous with state verbs. State verbs are verbs that:
- describe feelings (e.g. like, love, hate, need, etc)
- express thoughts and opinions (e.g. know, think, want, understand, mean, etc)
- refer to the senses (e.g. see, hear, smell, taste)
- express possession (e.g. belong, have, etc)

1 Choose the correct option to complete the sentences.

1 I'm working at the park …
   a) at the moment.   b) every summer.
2 I usually work for two months …
   a) at the moment.   b) every summer.
3 Why do you want to be a teacher?
   a) Because I love kids.   b) Because I'm loving kids.
4 … at the moment?
   a) Do you study   b) Are you studying
5 Can I call you later? I … dinner.
   a) eat   b) am eating

2 Complete the sentences with the verbs in brackets in the present simple or present continuous.

1 Right now, I _____ (make) a sandwich for my little brother because he _____ (be) hungry.
2 What _____ you _____ (do)? Are you busy?
3 What _____ you _____ (do)? Are you an architect or an engineer?
4 I'm really busy this term. I _____ (study) and _____ (work) part time.
5 We usually _____ (drive) our car to work, but this week we _____ (cycle) because the weather is nice.
6 I _____ (understand) exactly what you _____ (say).

UNIT 7

CAN/CAN'T – ABILITY

Function
We use **can/can't** to talk about ability (things we know how to do or things we are good at).

Form
Subject + can/can't + base form

Affirmative/Negative

I/You/He/ She/It/We/ They	can	swim.
	can't/cannot	

Short answers

Yes,	I/you/he/she/ it/we/they	can.
No,		can't/cannot.

Yes/No questions

Can	I/you/he/she/it/we/they	swim?

1 Put the words in the correct order to form sentences. Use capital letters when necessary.

1 paint / brother / my / well / very / can
_____

2 ride / you / motorbike / can / a
_____ ?

3 the / I / guitar / play / can't
_____

4 cook / sister / I / can't / and / my
_____

5 French / can / speak / and / she / German
_____

2 Complete the conversation with *can* or *can't* and short answers, as appropriate.

George: Anna, _____ you ski?

Anna: _____. I love skiing!

George: Really? I _____ ski, but I want to learn.

Anna: Well, _____ you water ski?

George: _____, but I can windsurf.

Anna: Oh, I _____ windsurf, too. It's great!

ADVERBS OF MANNER

Function

Adverbs of manner refer to actions and describe how a person does an action. e.g. *I speak quickly. He can run fast.*

Form

adjective + *-ly*

We usually form the adverb by adding -ly to the adjective, e.g. *slow – slowly, quick – quickly, careful – carefully.*

Spelling rules:

- adjectives that end in -y, change the -y to -i and add -ly, e.g. *funny – funnily*
- adjectives that end in -e, drop the -e and add -ly. e.g. *true – truly* But: *unbelievable – unbelievably, comfortable – comfortably*

There are some irregular adverbs, e.g. *good – well, fast – fast.*

Adverbs usually come after the verb (subject + verb + adverb), e.g. *She can't dance well.*

1 Choose the correct option.

1 Kevin is a good / well singer.
2 I have to finish this project quick / quickly.
3 He can't cook very good / well.
4 I'm a really bad / badly dancer!
5 That guy can run really fast / fastly!
6 The kittens are playing happy / happily.

2 Complete the sentences with adverb forms of the adjectives from the box.

| quiet   noisy   good   slow   fast |

1 My mum can play the guitar really _____.
2 Can you speak more _____? I can't understand you.
3 Shhh! Please work _____ and don't talk.
4 The children are playing _____. I can't hear the TV!
5 We don't have much time, so we need to work _____.

UNIT 8

THIS, THAT, THESE, THOSE

Form

this/that + singular noun
these/those + plural noun

Function

We use **this** and **these** to talk about things that are close to the person who is speaking.

We use **that** and **those** to talk about things that are not very close to the person who is speaking.

1 Choose the correct option.

1 I don't like the colour of that / those jacket.
2 Are this / these jeans a size ten?
3 Look at that / those nice shorts!
4 How much is this / those cap?
5 Give me this / that shirt, please. I can't reach it.

2 Look at the pictures. Complete the sentences with *this*, *that*, *these*, and *those*.

 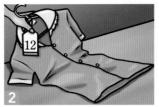  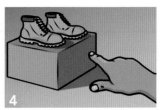

1   I don't like _____ trousers. They're really old!

2   _____ shirt is too big. Do you have a size 8?

3   I really like _____ jacket. I'd like to try it on.

4   _____ boots are cool. I like them.

COMPARATIVE ADJECTIVES

Function
We use comparative adjectives to compare two things or people.

Form
Comparative adjectives have one form. They do not change if the noun is singular or plural.
Spelling rules:
- one-syllable adjectives add -er, e.g. *small – smaller, short – shorter*
- one-syllable adjectives ending in -e, add -r, e.g. *safe – safer, rude – ruder*
- one-syllable adjectives ending consonant-vowel-consonant, double the final consonant and add -er, e.g. *fat – fatter, thin – thinner*
- two-syllable adjectives ending in -y, change the -y to -i and add -er
  e.g. *happy – happier, funny – funnier*
- adjectives with two or more syllables, use more/less to form the comparative,
  e.g. *interesting – more interesting, popular – less popular*

Irregular comparatives: *good – better, bad – worse*

Noun + be + comparative adjective + than + noun, e.g. *Sofia is **taller than** Joseph.*

1 Write the comparative form of these adjectives.

1 beautiful _____	4 practical _____	7 hot _____
2 pretty _____	5 big _____	8 cool _____
3 nice _____	6 crazy _____	

2 Complete the sentences with the correct comparative form of the adjective in brackets. Pay attention to the arrows indicating more or less.

1   I think Justin Bieber is _____ Justin Timberlake. (↑ famous)

2   Is this skirt _____ that dress? (↑ casual)

3   My new MP3 player is _____ my old one. (↑ compact)

4   My cat is _____ my dog! (↑ fat)

5   This jumper is _____ that one. (↓ expensive)

UNIT 9

COUNTABLE AND UNCOUNTABLE NOUNS WITH *SOME, ANY, MUCH, MANY*

Form
Countable nouns are nouns you can count. They have singular and plural forms. *e.g. orange – oranges*
Uncountable nouns are nouns you can't count. They don't have a plural form. *e.g. bread, meat, cheese*

Countable nouns	Singular	Plural	Uncountable nouns
Affirmative	I want **a** sandwich.	I want **some** sandwiches.	I want **some** cheese.
Negative	I don't want **a** sandwich.	I don't want **any** sandwiches. There aren't **many** potatoes.	I don't want **any** cheese. There isn't **much** bread.
Questions	Do you want **a** sandwich?	Do you want **any** sandwiches? How **many** oranges do you have?	Do you want **any** cheese? How **much** butter is there?

1 Write these words in the correct category.

| meat | bread | potato | apple | bean | soup | fruit | orange | cheese | sandwich | yoghurt | strawberry |

Countable nouns	Uncountable nouns

2 Complete the sentences with *some, any, much, many.*

1 I'm hungry. I want _____ crackers.
2 I'd like _____ water, please.
3 How _____ juice do we have?
4 Do we have _____ coffee?
5 I don't want _____ dessert. I don't like sweet food.
6 Oh, look. There are _____ good shops in this city.

VERB PHRASES

Form/Function

Expressing wishes and desires	I would like / 'd like to … I would love / 'd love to … I want to …	e.g. I'd love to go to the cinema tonight. I want to go to the theatre on Saturday.
Making invitations	Do you want to …? Would you like to …?	e.g. Do you want to go to the cinema tonight? Would you like to go to the theatre on Saturday?
Making suggestions	Let's … Shall we …	e.g. Let's go to the cinema tonight. Shall we go to the theatre on Saturday?
Expressing obligation and necessity	I have to … I need to …	e.g. I have to be at home at 6 tonight. I need to call James tomorrow.

1 Tick (✓) the correct sentences. Correct the sentences which have mistakes.

1 I'd love see that film.
_____

2 Would you like going out to dinner tonight?
_____

3 Do you want to watch TV?
_____

4 A: Would you love to go to the zoo? B: Yes, I'd love to!
_____

5 Shall we to meet at seven?
_____

6 We would like to try the new Greek restaurant.
_____

2 Complete the conversation with appropriate verb phrases. In some cases, more than one answer is possible.

Liam: OK, guys. What (1) _____ you _____ to do tonight?
Greg: I (2) _____ see that new horror film. It's almost Halloween!
Nancy: Ugh! I don't (3) _____ see a horror film!
Katie: And I (4) _____ study tonight. I have an exam on Monday.
Liam: Today is Friday! (5) _____ you _____ study tonight?
Katie: Yes. I (6) _____ study tonight if I (7) _____ get a good mark.
Nancy: OK. (8) _____ we go out tomorrow night then?
Liam: Sure. (9) _____ meet at Paolo's Pizza at 7.30.

PAST SIMPLE – AFFIRMATIVE STATEMENTS

Function
We use the past simple to talk about states, events, actions, experiences in the past.

Form
To form the past simple:
- with most verbs add -ed, e.g. *answer – answered, listen – listened, walk – walked, want – wanted*
- with verbs ending in -e, add -d, e.g. *prepare – prepared, like – liked, loved – loved*
- with verbs ending in consonant -y, change the -y to -i and add -ed, e.g. *study – studied, try – tried*
- with one-syllable verbs ending in vowel-single consonant, double the consonant and add -ed, e.g. *stop – stopped, plan – planned*
- with two-syllable verbs ending in a vowel-single consonant, if the stress is on the last syllable, double the consonant and add -ed, e.g. refer – referred But: *offer – offered, travel – travelled*

Irregular past forms: e.g. *go – went, eat – ate, be – was/were …*
For the full list of irregular verbs, see page 168.

1 Write the past simple forms of these verbs in the correct column.

| live   visit   see   watch   go   have   do   carry   stay   take   study   read   be   like |

Regular past tense verbs   Irregular past tense verbs

1 _____   1 _____

2 _____   2 _____

3 _____   3 _____

4 _____   4 _____

5 _____   5 _____

6 _____   6 _____

7 _____   7 _____

2 Complete the paragraph with past tense verbs from the list above.

Last weekend, I (1) _____ to the history museum with my family. It (2) _____
really interesting because I learnt a lot of things about the history of my city.
I (3) _____ national history in secondary school, but not local history. In the
museum, we (4) _____ exhibits of life here in the 19th century. People's lives
(5) _____ difficult in those days! They (6) _____ in simple houses with no
water or electricity. They (7) _____ water to their houses, and they (8) _____
books by candle light at night. I'm happy that I live in the 21st century!

PAST SIMPLE – QUESTIONS AND NEGATIVE STATEMENTS

Form
To form the negative, questions and short answers in the past simple, we use the auxiliary
verb *did* (but not with the verb *be*).

	be	Other verbs
Negative	Subject + *wasn't/weren't* The food **wasn't** very good. The chairs **weren't** very comfortable.	Subject + *didn't* + base form The menu **didn't have** a very big selection.
Yes/No questions	*Was/Were* + subject …? **Was** it expensive? **Were** the bathrooms clean?	*Did* + subject + base form …? **Did** you **like** Brennan's?

Short answers	*Yes,* + subject + *was/were.* *No,* + subject + *wasn't/weren't.* Yes, it **was**. / No, it **wasn't**. Yes, they **were**. / No, they **weren't**.	*Yes,* + subject + *did. /* *No,* + subject + *didn't.* Yes, I **did**. / No, I **didn't**.
Information questions	*Wh*-question word + *was/were* + subject …? **How was** your weekend? **What were** the people like?	*Wh*-question word + *did* + subject + base form …? **What did** you **do** at the weekend? **Where did** you **go**?

1 Choose the correct word.

1 How did / was your weekend?
2 Were / Did you have fun at the party? Yes, I was / did.
3 I didn't like / liked the film.
4 Where did you go / went after school yesterday?
5 The party didn't / wasn't fun.

2 Complete the conversation with correct forms of the verbs in parentheses.

Peter: What (1) _____ you _____ (*do*) on your holiday, Maddy?
Maddy: We (2) _____ (*stay*) at home and painted our house. It (3) _____ (*be*) fun!
Peter: What colour (4) _____ you _____ (*paint*) it?
Maddy: Well, we (5) _____ (*not want*) to paint it a boring colour, so we painted it yellow.
Peter: Yellow! Well, that definitely isn't boring!

UNIT 11

PAST SIMPLE WITH *WHEN* CLAUSES

Form

when clause	Main clause	
When Steve was older,	he learnt to work with crocodiles.	Use a comma.

Main clause	*when* clause	
Steve learnt to work with crocodiles	**when** he was older.	Don't use a comma.

Function
The action in the *when* clause happened at the same time or before the other event in the sentence.

1 Match 1–5 with a–e to complete the sentences.

1 When Henry Ford moved to Detroit,
2 When Marie and Pierre got married
3 Steve Jobs entered Reed College
4 When Ray Tomlinson invented email,
5 Manufacturing changed

a) when he finished high school.
b) he decided to use the @ symbol.
c) he got a job as a machinist.
d) when Ford invented the assembly line.
e) they began to work together.

2 Rewrite these sentences using *when* clauses to combine them. Think about which event happened first.

1 I woke up. I saw my birthday present.
2 I got a surprise email. I logged on.
3 My sister got a job as an architect. She graduated from university.
4 I was happy. I passed my exam.
5 My mother was born. Her family moved to Glasgow.

SUBJECT AND OBJECT PRONOUNS

Form

Subject pronouns	I	you	he	she	it	we	you	they
Object pronouns	me	you	him	her	it	us	you	them

Function

Subject and object pronouns replace proper names and nouns.

DIRECT AND INDIRECT OBJECTS

Form

Subject	+ verb	+ person/thing (object)	
Helen	met	**Stuart**	in the centre.
Helen	met	**him**	in the centre.

Some verbs can take two objects, a person (**indirect object**) and a thing (**direct object**). The thing is usually the **direct object** and the person is usually the **indirect object**.

Subject	+ verb	+ person (indirect object)	+ thing (direct object)
She	gave	me	a flower.
He	bought	Kathy/her	a present.

or

Subject	+ verb	+ thing (direct object)	+ preposition	+ person (indirect object)
The indirect object always comes after the preposition.				
She	gave	it	to	me.
He	bought	a present/it	for	her.

1 **Rewrite the sentences, replacing the <u>underlined</u> words with pronouns.**

1   In primary school, my favourite teacher was Ms Watkins. I liked <u>Ms Watkins</u> very much.
    she

2   I bought a new mobile phone yesterday. I got <u>the mobile phone</u> on sale.
    it

3   My parents gave <u>my brother</u> <u>some new boots</u> for his birthday.
    They   to him   them

4   My family and I ate at a new restaurant yesterday. <u>My family and I</u> liked <u>the restaurant</u>.
    We like it

5   We met <u>Will</u> in the park last week. We talked to <u>Will</u> about <u>our holiday plans</u>.
    We met him, we talk about them

2 **Each sentence has a mistake in the use of direct or indirect objects. Rewrite the sentences correctly.**

1   My parents to me gave their old car.
    My parents gave to me their old car.

2   Sarah saw to John in the supermarket.
    Sarah saw John in the supermarket

3   Our teacher explained us object pronouns.
    Our teacher explained object to us pronouns.

4   My brother won a prize. It won him in a spelling competition. *My brother won a prize. He won her in a spelling competition*

5   We bought a present him.
    We bought a present for him.

UNIT 12

PRESENT CONTINUOUS AS FUTURE

Function

We can use the present continuous to talk about definite plans and arrangements in the future.
e.g. *A: What are you doing this weekend? B: I'm meeting some friends.*

1 **Choose the correct option.**

1 What are you doing tomorrow?
   a) I go on holiday.   b) I'm flying to Madrid.
2 What are you doing this evening?
   a) I want to go to the cinema.   b) I'm wanting to go to the cinema.
3 It's my birthday tomorrow.
   a) Do you come to my party?   b) Are you coming to my party?
4 A: _____ B: Yes, we are.
   a) Are you moving house next year?   b) Do you move house next year?
5 Do you have any plans for the evening?
   a) Yes, I'm having dinner with my friend.   b) Yes, I have dinner with my friend.

2 **Complete the sentences with past, present or future (present continuous) tenses of the verbs in brackets.**

1 Last weekend _was_ (be) really boring, but next weekend, I _going_ (go) to a good party.
2 I almost never _go_ (go) out on weekdays, but this Thursday I _'m meeting_ (meet) with friends for dinner.
3 When _is_ that new department store _opening_ (open)? I _want_ (want) to go there.
4 My parents _giving_ (give) me a car for my graduation present next month!
5 I _'m going_ (go) running after school. _Do_ you _want_ (want) to come with me?

GOING TO

Function

We use **going to** to talk about plans and intentions in the future.

Form

Subject + be + going to + base form

Affirmative	I'm going to improve my English.
Negative	We're not going to have a test next week.
Questions	Is Victor going to study tomorrow? Yes, he is. / No, he isn't.
	What are you going to do tonight?

1 **Complete the conversation with correct forms of be + going to.**

Sandy: I don't have any money! I (1) _going to get_ (get) a job!
Kyle: I think my dad (2) _____ (give) me a job in his shop this summer.
Sandy: Really? What (3) _____ you _____ (do)?
Kyle: I (4) _____ (answer) phone calls.
Sandy: Oh. That (5) _____ (not be) very interesting.
Kyle: No, it isn't, but it's a job. I need the money.
Sandy: Yeah, that's true. You're lucky.
Kyle: Yes, I am. It's not a great job, but I (6) _____ (complain)!

2 **In which sentences can you replace 'going to' with the present continuous form? Rewrite the sentences that can use the present continuous.**

1 I want to do more exercise – I'm <u>going to cycle</u> to work more often.

_____

2 Peter loves photography. He's <u>going to go</u> shopping for a new camera tomorrow.

_____

3 I don't like how she speaks to me. I'm <u>going to tell</u> her how I feel.

_____

4 My friend from Australia is <u>going to visit</u> next week.

_____

5 I'm <u>going to meet</u> my friends at the cinema tonight.

_____

Irregular verbs

Infinitive	Past simple	Past participle
be	was/were	been
become	became	become
begin	began	begun
break	broke	broken
bring	brought	brought
build	built	built
buy	bought	bought
catch	caught	caught
choose	chose	chosen
come	came	come
cost	cost	cost
cut	cut	cut
do	did	done
draw	drew	drawn
drink	drank	drunk
drive	drove	driven
eat	ate	eaten •
fall	fell	fallen
feed	fed	fed
feel	felt	felt
find	found	found
fly	flew	flown
get	got	got
give	gave	given
go	went	gone
grow	grew	grown
hang	hung	hung
have	had	had
hear	heard	heard
hit	hit	hit
hold	held	held
hurt	hurt	hurt
keep	kept	kept
know	knew	known
learn	learnt	learnt
leave	left	left
let	let	let
lose	lost	lost
make	made	made
meet	met	met
pay	paid	paid
put	put	put
read	read	read
ride	rode	ridden
ring	rang	rung
rise	rose	risen
run	ran	run
say	said	said
see	saw	seen
sell	sold	sold
send	sent	sent
set	set	set
sing	sang	sung
sit	sat	sat
speak	spoke	spoken
stand	stood	stood
stick	stuck	stuck
take	took	taken
teach	taught	taught
tell	told	told
think	thought	thought
throw	threw	thrown
understand	understood	understood
wake	woke	woken
wear	wore	worn
win	won	won
write	wrote	written

Pronunciation symbols

Vowels

ɪ	did
e	bed, neck
æ	bad, hand
ɒ	box
ʌ	but, mother
ʊ	book, good
ə	banana, computer
iː	feed
ɑː	father
ɔː	tall
uː	boot, food, student
ɜː	shirt, birthday
eɪ	date, table
aɪ	cry, eye
ɔɪ	boy
əʊ	comb, post
aʊ	about, how
ʊə	tour
eə	their
ɪə	here, near

Consonants

p	park, happy
b	back, hobby
t	tea
d	die
k	came, kitchen, quarter
g	game, go
f	face, photographer
v	vegetable
θ	thing, maths
ð	then, that
s	city, summer
z	please, goes
ʃ	she, shop
ʒ	leisure
h	hot, who
tʃ	chicken, watch
dʒ	jacket, orange
m	men
n	sun, know
ŋ	sung, singer
w	week, white
r	rain, writer
l	light, long
j	yes, use, music

Audioscript

UNIT 1 Nice to meet you!

05

Hi. This is Carla. Where are you? Anyway, listen – it's my birthday soon! It's on 18ᵗʰ August. Come to my party! It's at the Clinton Club in town. That's C-L-I-N-T-O-N. The party is at nine. Call me, OK? Bye!

06

1

Receptionist:	Thank you, Mr Mahuad. Oh, what's your departure date?
Mr Mahuad:	Departure date?
R:	The day you leave the hotel.
Mr M:	Oh, 21ˢᵗ June.
R:	That's fine. Thank you.

2

Yousef:	I'm sorry. Can you help me with this?
Woman:	Sure. What's the problem?
Y:	What is the security code?
W:	It's a number on the back of your card. Here.
Y:	Oh, yes. 624. Thank you very much.
W:	You're welcome.

UNIT 2 What do you do?

09

Hi. I'm Sarah. I'm a doctor. Will is my brother. He's a firefighter. Here is Cathy. She's my mum. She's a teacher. This is my dad, Robert. He's a taxi driver. Cathy and Robert are my parents. His mum is Rose. She's my grandma. And Brian is my granddad. That's my family! And here is James. He's a police officer. He's my boyfriend.

10

1   Cathy and Robert are my parents. Will and I are their children.
2   Will is my brother. I'm his sister.
3   Cathy's my mum and Robert is my dad. I am their daughter and Will is their son.
4   James is my boyfriend. I am his girlfriend.
5   Rose and Brian are my grandparents. Will and I are their grandchildren.
6   Robert is my dad. Cathy is his wife. Robert is her husband.

11

My name is Rachel Hughes, and I'm a teacher. I work in a large secondary school. My job is very difficult, but I love it. I work from Monday to Friday. My day usually starts at eight o'clock. I leave school at four o'clock and then I work at home. My husband has a difficult job, too. He's a firefighter!

12

Rachel:	Hi, Lisa! How are you?
Lisa:	I'm great, Rachel. Good to see you!
R:	You too! What do you do now?
L:	Well, I'm a lawyer.
R:	Wow! Really?
L:	Yes. I work in an office. It's not far from here.
R:	Do you like your job?
L:	It's very interesting.
R:	And what about your sister, Jane?
L:	Oh, she's fine. She's a doctor now.
R:	Fantastic! Let's meet for coffee some time.
L:	Great idea!

UNIT 3 Down time

17

Amy:	Hello, I'm Amy. Welcome to Gaming World, the show that's all about video games. This week, I have Angelica and Victor with me.
Angelica and Victor:	Hi.
Am:	Now, Angelica, what games do you like?
An:	Well, I play football and tennis games.
Am:	And you, Victor?
V:	I prefer games with more action. I don't really play sports or puzzle games.
Am:	So what do you think of this week's game, Automania?
V:	I play a lot of driving games, and this one is very good. It has a lot of action and the story is great.
Am:	And how about you, Angelica? Do you feel the same as Victor?
An:	Yes, well, I don't play driving games. But this game has a lot of action, and I like the story.
Am:	Okay, thank you both very much for your opinions.

18

Oswaldo:	So Jenny, what films do you like?
Jenny:	Well, I really like love stories. I think they're great. And you?
O:	I don't really like love stories. I think they're boring. I prefer action films. Hey, Caroline, what's your opinion?
Caroline:	Um, I don't like love stories or action films. I love science-fiction films!
O:	Really? How about you, Andy?
Andy:	I like things that are funny, so comedies are my favourite.

UNIT 4 Day in, day out

22

What's your daily routine? Here's what one person says about her week.

Interviewer:	Um, what's your daily routine?
Woman:	Well, on Mondays I work in the office. On Tuesdays, I have a class after work. On Wednesdays, I go to the gym before work. That gives me energy for the rest of the week! On Thursdays, I usually meet friends for coffee.
I:	And Friday?
W:	There's a dance class I usually go to on Friday evenings. On Saturdays, I relax at home and watch TV.

23

Interviewer:	Tell me about Sundays. What do you do on Sundays?
Woman:	I usually get up late and have breakfast. I often read the newspaper at the same time. In the late morning, I usually go for a walk in the park. I get home and I have lunch at one.
I:	What about after lunch?
W:	In the early afternoon, I do the housework. The rest of the day, I cook and relax.

24

Eve:	So, Owen. What do you do when you're not at university?
Owen:	I usually have a very busy week. I do different activities almost every evening.
E:	Really? What activities do you do?
O:	Well, I go in-line skating twice a week. And I have an art class on Wednesday evenings.
E:	An art class? That's interesting!
O:	Why don't you come along next week?
E:	Sounds fun. And what do you usually do at the weekend?
O:	I go hang-gliding on Saturday. Do you want to come along to try that?
E:	No way! Art class is exciting enough for me!

UNIT 5   Here, there and everywhere

25

Hello and welcome to our phone guide for this year's Chinese New Year festival. There's a lot for everyone to enjoy. Between January 23rd and 28th there's a special exhibition of Chinese paintings at the art gallery on Park Street. There are special events at the zoo for children under 10 and Chinese dancers and musicians in the park every day at 11am. Chinese food is available from special stalls at the shopping centre at weekends. Please note that there are special buses which leave hourly from the bus station …

27

Now, everyone likes a food fight. In the town of Buñol, they have perhaps the biggest food fight in the world. Buñol is near Valencia in Spain. They have a tomato festival called La Tomatina. It happens in August and everyone in the town throws tomatoes. About 30,000 people enjoy this festival every year.

28

Presenter:	We sent our reporter, Mary Turner, to Buñol to learn more about the festival.
Reporter:	Right now, there are more than 30,000 people here in Buñol, with people from Britain, Germany and other countries. That's because today is the day of La Tomatina, the tomato festival. I want to ask local people about the festival. Excuse me …
Spanish man:	Yes?
R:	I'm from Channel Ten news. Are you from Buñol?
Sp man:	Yes. I live here.
R:	What happens in La Tomatina?
Sp man:	Well, everyone goes to the main square to have breakfast. At 11 o'clock, everyone starts throwing tomatoes at each other.
R:	And how long does it last?
Sp man:	We throw the tomatoes for about two hours. The whole town is red at the end!
R:	And why do you do it?
Sp man:	I don't know! It's just for fun!

UNIT 6   Different strokes

32

1   Yeah, sure. My date of birth is 27th April, 1992.
2   Give me a call on Saturday on 210-3784-611.
3   The flight leaves at 7.35 in the morning.
4   You need to be 18 years or over to enter the club.
5   This restaurant dates from 1925.

33

1   Hi, this is Tom Edwards. Does anyone remember me? Class of 1997? I'm currently working in Germany.
    I'm planning to go to the school reunion in March.
    Er, yeah 18th March. My birthday! Hope to see you then.
2   Hello. It's me, Paul Newton. I'm hoping to travel back from Sydney, Australia, for the school reunion. It's happening on 14th August this year. Are you going too? Then please call me on 0061-342-8932. Thanks!
3   This is Vanessa Hughes. I'm teaching at Glendale School right now. There's a school reunion for all students from the year 2002. It's at 7.30 on 9th April 2012 in the school hall. Everyone is invited to come. See you there!

UNIT 7   You've got talent!

38

Jonathan:	Hello?
Jenny:	Hi, Jonathan. It's Jenny. Listen, Carmen Dean is applying for a job as an English teacher at a language institute. I'm writing a personal reference for her. Can you help me?
Jon:	Of course.
J:	OK, so I need to list at least three qualities that make Carmen a good candidate for a job as a teacher. What qualities do you think she has?
Jon:	That's easy! First, Carmen is really friendly. She likes meeting new people, and she loves talking to people.
J:	That's true. She is really friendly, and that's important for a teacher. What else?
Jon:	Well, she's very organised and reliable. She's good at making plans, and people can depend on her.
J:	Yeah, that's good. Organised … and reliable. Anything else?
Jon:	Yeah, you know, Carmen is also very patient. She's helping me with my Spanish, and she often explains things several times!
J:	Great! That's all I need. Thanks, Jonathan!
Jon:	You're welcome. I hope Carmen gets the job!

41

Cindy:	So, Mike, what show are you reviewing this week?
Mike:	This week it's *Dream Stars* – the new TV talent show.
C:	Another TV talent show!
M:	Yes, but you know what? I love it! OK, some of the contestants in the singing competition can't sing very well, but most of them are quite good. My favourite section is the dance competition because all of those kids can really dance! In fact, some of them also compete on that American show *Can You Dance?*
C:	Oh, yes, that's a great show! OK, and what about the competition for comedians? Most comedians can't make me laugh. What about these?
M:	Well, I don't know about you, but most of the comedians on *Dream Stars* can certainly make me laugh!

43

1   Really? That's amazing! Me, too!
2   Wow! Really?
3   Oh, how interesting!

45

A: Can I help you?
B: Yes, please. I'd like to try on this jacket.
A: Sure. Is that one the right size?
B: No, it's too small. Do you have it in a size 10?
A: Yes, here's a 10.
B: Thanks. How much is it?
A: It's fifty pounds.
B: OK, I'll take it.
A: Would you like to try on anything else?
B: No, thank you. Here's my credit card.

46

1 one thousand, five hundred dollars
2 three hundred and eighty-five yen
3 ten pence
4 one hundred and twenty-seven thousand, three hundred and ninety-five euros
5 twelve thousand, four hundred pounds
6 fifty cents

47

1 A: Can I have five hundred and sixty dollars from this account, please?
   B: Certainly. How do you want that?
   A: Erm, in twenties, please.
2 C: How much is this bag?
   D: It's nine hundred and ninety-nine yen.
   C: Wow! That's a good price!
3 E: We'd like to buy this flat, but it's two hundred and thirty-five thousand, four hundred and fifty euros.
   F: Well, I can speak to the owner and maybe he can lower the price for you.
   E: That would be great!
4 G: Seventeen pounds sixty-eight? OK. Can I pay by credit card?
   H: Yes, you can.
   G: Good.

48

1 At Burger Bar we know you want good food at a great price. That's why our Fun Meal comes with a burger, chips and soft drink, for only four pounds and ninety-nine pence. Put a smile on your face at Burger Bar today.
2 You want a phone? You want an MP3 player? You want a handheld computer? You want it all, right? Which means all you really need is three hundred and fifty pounds and the SMax 750 can be yours.
3 Not many people in the world have two hundred and twenty thousand pounds to spend on a car. Not many cars in the world have a top speed of nearly 200 kilometres an hour. The new Ferris Avenger. For the lion in you.
4 There are people who say a watch is just a watch. But then, they probably don't own an 18-karat gold Monarch Supreme. Women who do own one know that at nine thousand, seven hundred pounds it's the best gift that money can buy.

51

1
Woman: Good morning, Tina Baker's office.
John: Hi. This is John. Could I speak to Tina, please?
W: I'm sorry, she isn't in. May I take a message?
J: Yes. Please ask her to meet me at Dan's Burgers at 12.30.
W: Meet John at Dan's Burgers at 12.30.

J: That's right. Thank you.
W: You're welcome.
2
Woman: Hello?
Lauren: Hi, is Ryan there, please?
W: No, he isn't. Do you want to leave a message?
L: Yeah. This is Lauren. Please tell him that dinner is on Friday, March 30th.
W: Friday, March 30th?
L: Yes. And can you ask him to call me?
W: Sure.
L: Thanks.
W: You're welcome.

52

Lisa: Hello?
Eric: Hi, this is Eric. Is Emily there?
L Hi, Eric, this is Lisa. Emily isn't here. Do you want to leave a message?
E: Oh, yes, can you tell her to meet me at the restaurant at eight o'clock?
L: Sure, restaurant, eight o'clock, right?
E: That's right. Thanks, Lisa.
L: No problem. Bye.
E: Bye.

59

end – ended
work – worked
explain – explained
practise – practised
hate – hated
stay – stayed

61

1
Woman: Oh, hi, Alex! How was your holiday?
Man: Oh, it was terrible!
W: Oh no! Why?
M: We went on a tour of Hawaii, but it wasn't fun. The tour guide wasn't very friendly, and he didn't give us much information about the Hawaiian Islands.
W: Oh, it's a shame the guide wasn't good.
M: Yeah, he was terrible. I complained to the tour company.
W: I'm sorry you didn't have fun.
2
Man: How was your weekend, Karen?
Woman: It was fantastic!
M: Oh, good! What did you do?
W: Well, my boyfriend took me out for dinner on Friday night. We went to a really nice French restaurant, and the food was excellent.
   On Saturday my friend and I went to the fair and it was really fun. On Sunday my boyfriend and I saw a really good film. So it was a fun weekend.
M: Good. You were really tired on Friday, so I'm glad you had a good weekend.
W: Thanks.

UNIT 11 Great lives

63

Audrey Hepburn was born on 4th May 1929, in Brussels, Belgium. Her career as an actress began in London in 1948, but she moved to New York when she was only 22 to become a Broadway actress. Soon after that, Hepburn began acting in Hollywood films, and she quickly became very, very famous. She won her first Oscar® in 1953 when she was only 24 years old, and she won many more awards during her career. Hepburn's last film was *Always*, directed by Steven Spielberg, in 1989. She decided to end her acting career because she wanted to help children around the world. She worked with UNICEF and travelled to many countries in Asia, Africa, and Latin America. She died at her home in Switzerland on 20th January 1993. Audrey Hepburn was a great actress and a great humanitarian.

UNIT 12 In the near future

70

Rick:	So where are you going on holiday, Charlie?
Charlie:	Thailand.
R:	Thailand? Wow! Cool!
C:	I know. I'm really excited. I'm going on a tour of Buddhist temples.
R:	A what?!
C:	A tour of temples. I'm going to see the most famous Buddhist temples in Thailand.
R:	Oh. Well, that's great, I suppose. Are some of those temples near beaches? Thailand has some of the best beaches in the world, you know.
C:	Uh, yeah, I think so. I'm not really going to beaches though.
R:	Not going to beaches? No beaches? Seriously?
C:	Yes, seriously. You know I'm studying architecture. I don't have much time, and I want to see as many different temples as possible.
R:	Wow, well, whatever. Have a fantastic time on that tour. Me? I'm going to Greece, but not to look at old buildings. I'm going to the beach!

71

go swimming, go running, go horse riding, go walking, go dancing, go cycling, go shopping

Grammar Review answer key

1	1	is
	2	is
	3	are
	4	is
	5	are
	6	are
2	1	Their
	2	My
	3	Its
	4	Her
	5	His
	6	your
3	1	is
	2	are; pens
	3	is
	4	are
	5	is
	6	is
4	1	a
	2	an
	3	– (no article)
	4	the
	5	The
	6	the
	7	an
5	1	Who
	2	How
	3	Where
	4	What
	5	What
	6	When
6	1	How do you pronounce your surname?
	2	Where is your sister's husband from?
	3	Can you speak Italian?
	4	What time does your lesson finish?
	5	What do you have for lunch?
	6	Does Kelly like her job?

7	1	can't speak
	2	can cook
	3	can ride
	4	can't ride
	5	can't cook
	6	can speak
8	1	Does, D
	2	Are, A
	3	Is, F
	4	Does, B
	5	Do, C
	6	Do, E
9	1	are not
	2	doesn't like
	3	work
	4	don't have
	5	finishes
	6	goes
10	1	He's = His
	2	Katya = Katya's
	3	Ours = Our
	4	parents friend's = parents' friends
	5	Michaels = Michael's
	6	Hers = Her
11	1	nickname's Dev
	2	They're not
	3	time's
	4	Martin's
	5	*no contraction possible*
	6	When's
	7	*no contraction possible*
	8	There's
12	1	usually checks
	2	rarely drink
	3	always watches
	4	sometimes get up
	5	often writes
	6	never spend

Language wrap-up answer key

UNIT 1

1 Vocabulary

A
1 help
2 say
3 slowly
4 spell
5 repeat

B
1 23rd
2 14th
3 1st
4 5th
5 2nd

2 Grammar
1 is
2 am
3 is
4 am
5 are
6 are
7 How old
8 When
9 Where
10 What

UNIT 2

1 Vocabulary
1 parents
2 dad
3 wife
4 sisters
5 brother
6 soldier
7 officer
8 daughter
9 grandparents
10 driver

2 Grammar

A
1 a
2 –
3 an
4 an
5 the

B
1 Whose
2 his
3 Clooney's
4 mine
5 children's

UNIT 3

1 Vocabulary

A
1 go online
2 listen to
3 play sports
4 see friends
5 watch TV

B
1 e   4 d
2 a   5 c
3 b

2 Grammar
1 do, know
2 plays
3 do, do
4 study
5 work
6 has
7 Do, like
8 don't want
9 doesn't think
10 does, want

UNIT 4

Vocabulary

A
1 go, quarter past eight
2 have, seven (o'clock)
3 go, half past ten

B
1 before
2 after
3 On, until

Grammar

A
1 Leo
2 David
3 Marina
4 Samuel
5 Lola

B
1 Leo has dinner before he plays games on his computer.
2 Marina chats to friends online until it's time for bed.
3 David plays video games after he does his homework.
4 Lola watches TV until she goes to bed.
5 Samuel listens to music after he plays a video game.

UNIT 5

1 Vocabulary

A
1 art gallery
2 science museum
3 shopping centre
4 police station

B
1 on/in, over, science museum, next to
2 police station, opposite

2 Grammar
1 is
2 lots of
3 is
4 don't
5 are
6 stay
7 Don't
8 many
9 a lot of
10 are

UNIT 6

1 Vocabulary

A
1 unhealthy
2 exciting
3 stressful
4 wasteful

B
1 save
2 lights
3 cycle
4 get
5 organic
6 reuse

2 Grammar
1 don't know
2 'm/am reading
3 knows
4 are destroying
5 need
6 work
7 cycle
8 'm/am working
9 don't agree
10 are learning

UNIT 7

1 Vocabulary
1 generous
2 cook
3 patient
4 sing
5 speak
6 clever
7 play
8 optimistic
9 honest
10 drive

2 Grammar
1 Can Francesca dance well?
No, she can't dance well.
2 Can your sister sing?
No, she sings very badly.
3 Can you swim fast?
No, I can't swim fast.

B run very fastly = run very fast
she comes quick = she comes quickly
She cans speak = She can speak
speak cat language very good = speak cat language very well

UNIT 8

1 Vocabulary

A
1 jumper
2 trainers
3 T-shirt
4 dress
5 skirt

B
1 cheap
2 attractive
3 user-friendly
4 powerful
5 expensive

2 Grammar
1 these
2 nicer
3 less expensive
4 this
5 better
6 those
7 prettier
8 easier
9 that
10 more interesting

UNIT 9

1 Vocabulary
1 soup
2 mushrooms
3 fried
4 salad
5 green
6 sparkling
7 bread
8 dessert
9 tart
10 chocolate

2 Grammar

A
1 Would you like to come
2 I'd like to cook
3 shall we watch
4 I need to get up
5 I have to go

B
1 some
2 some
3 olives
4 any
5 much

UNIT 10

1 Vocabulary
1 took a trip
2 amazing
3 got a fantastic gift
4 excited
5 got a special letter
6 surprised
7 saw a concert
8 tiring
9 met a famous person
10 interesting

2 Grammar

1 arrived
2 took
3 went
4 were
5 met
6 had
7 didn't stay
8 was
9 did, do
10 wasn't

UNIT 11

1 Vocabulary

1 wrote
2 discovered
3 graduated
4 got married
5 retired
6 composed
7 grew up
8 explored
9 had
10 built

2 Grammar

A 1 The athletes thanked them.
2 He won it in the 100 m.
3 I saved it for you.
4 I wrote a short biography about her.
5 I like to read about him.

B 1 I was very happy when my girlfriend sent me a postcard from Paris.
2 We were really surprised when Joanna and Marcus invited us over for dinner.
3 When the teacher gave George an A for his history exam, he was really excited.
4 When Anna's husband gave her a nice gift, she hugged him.

UNIT 12

1 Vocabulary

A 1 cycling
2 swimming
3 dancing
4 running
5 walking

B 1 start studying
2 stop eating fast food
3 start exercising
4 stop worrying
5 start going out

2 Grammar

A 1 is having
2 are visiting
3 is working
4 is meeting
5 are having

B 1 are, going to do
2 'm/am going to relax
3 'm/am not going to think
4 'm/am going to read
5 is going to take

Grammar Reference answer key

UNIT 1

1 1 is
2 are
3 not
4 aren't
5 isn't
6 am
7 Is
8 Are

2 1 c
2 e
3 b
4 d
5 a

1 1 is your name
2 Where
3 are they
4 When
5 Who
6 is your number

2 1 What is / What's your address?
2 How old are Richard and Mark?
3 When is / When's your birthday?
4 Who is / Who's your brother?
5 Where is / Where's our class?

UNIT 2

1 1 a, a
2 the, a
3 –, The
4 an, an
5 a, an

2 1 a   4 b
2 a   5 c
3 b

1 1 hasn't
2 Laura's
3 has
4 Smiths'
5 haven't
6 parents'

2 1 Whose are the books? They're theirs.
2 Whose is the pen? It's his.
3 Are they Amy's video games? No, they're ours.
4 Is he Pauls' brother? No, he's mine.
5 Whose is the jacket? It's hers.

UNIT 3

1 1 My brother like music and he downloads lots of songs. (likes)
2 Do Sarah have any interesting hobbies? (Does)
3 I love this song, but my girlfriend don't like it at all! (doesn't)

4 I doesn't buy many CDs, but I buy a lot of MP3s. (don't)
5 This sounds like a great song! Does you like it? (Do)
6 Does Simon plays the piano? Yes, he does. (play)

2 1 wakes
2 has
3 leaves
4 works
5 opens
6 don't have
7 serve
8 Does … like
9 doesn't pay
10 doesn't have

1 1 ✓
2 stays, stay
3 ✓
4 ✓
5 does, do

2 1 When does Will play golf?
2 Where do you work?
3 Why do Rafael and Mike arrive late every day?
4 Who does Leon look like?
5 What do I need for the meeting?

UNIT 4

1 1 is always
2 often think
3 Do … always catch
4 are never
5 rarely show
6 am sometimes

2 1 week   4 once
2 always   5 rarely
3 often

1 1 b   4 a
2 a   5 a
3 b   6 b

2 1 I finish studying before I call my friends. / Before I call my friends, I finish studying.
2 Olivia and Sara play tennis until they get tired and stop. / Until they get tired and stop, Olivia and Sara play tennis.
3 My wife does the washing up after I cook. / After I cook, my wife does the washing up.

4 The children play outside until it's time to eat. / Until it's time to eat, the children play outside.
5 I go bowling with my friends after I finish work. / After I finish work, I go bowling with my friends.
6 I go to the gym before I go to work. / Before I go to work, I go to the gym.

UNIT 5
1 1 Are there
  2 There is (There's)
  3 There a_____
  4 _____
  6 _____
2 1 many
  2 several 5 any
  3 a lot of
1 1 Don't get lost!
  2 Please sit down.
  3 Turn left at the traffic lights.
  4 Don't worry about the exam.
  5 Please don't talk during the film.
2 1 Turn
  2 be
  3 Don't run
  4 Walk
  5 don't watch
  6 Make

UNIT 6
1 1 running
  2 studying
  3 giving
  4 waiting
  5 swimming
  6 having
  7 worrying
  8 seeing
  9 sitting
  10 visiting
2 1 Are … coming; they are
  2 is … studying; is/'s studying
  3 Is … working; isn't; is/'s working
  4 Are … dating; I'm not
  5 is … talking; is/'s talking
1 1 a 4 b
  2 b 5 b
  3 a
2 1 'm making; is
  2 are … doing
  3 do … do
  4 'm studying; working

5 drive; are cycling
6 understand; are saying

UNIT 7
1 1 My brother can paint very well.
  2 Can you ride a motorbike?
  3 I can't play the guitar.
  4 My sister and I can't cook.
  5 She can speak French and German / German and French.
2 1 ca___
  2 Ye__ I can.
  3 can't
  4 can
     No, I can't
   ____
   ___ 4 bad
   __ 5 fast
   __ 6 happily
      noisily
   __ fast
   qu___

UNIT 8
1 1 that 4 this
  2 these 5 that
  3 those
2 1 these 3 that
  2 This 4 Those
1 1 more 5 bigger
     beautiful 6 crazier
  2 prettier 7 hotter
  3 nicer 8 cooler
  4 more practical
2 1 more famous than
  2 more casual than
  3 more compact than
  4 fatter than
  5 less expensive than

UNIT 9
1 Countable nouns: bean, potato, apple, orange, sandwich, strawberry
Uncountable nouns: meat, bread, soup, fruit, cheese, yoghurt
2 1 some 4 any
  2 some 5 any
  3 much 6 many
1 1 I'd love to see that film.
  2 Would you like to go out to dinner tonight?
  3 correct
  4 Would you like to go to the zoo?
  5 Shall we meet at seven?
  6 correct

2 1 do you want / would you like
  2 would like to / would love to / want to
  3 want to
  4 have to / need to
  5 Do you have to / need to
  6 have to / need to
  7 want to
  8 Shall
  9 Let's

UNIT 10
1 Regular verbs:
  1 lived
  2 visited
  3 watched
  4 carried
  5 stayed
  6 studied
  7 liked
Irregular verbs:
  1 saw 5 took
  2 went 6 read
  3 had 7 was/
  4 did were
2 1 went
  2 was
  3 studied
  4 saw
  5 were
  6 lived
  7 carried
  8 read
1 1 was 4 go
  2 Did 5 wasn't
  3 like
2 1 did you do
  2 stayed
  3 was
  4 did you paint
  5 didn't want

UNIT 11
1 1 c 4 b
  2 e 5 d
  3 a
2 1 When I woke up, I saw my birthday present. / I saw my birthday present when I woke up.
  2 When I logged on, I got a surprise email. / I got a surprise email when I logged on.
  3 My sister got a job as an architect when she graduated from university. / When she graduated from university, my sister got a job as an architect.
  4 I was happy when I passed my exam. /

When I passed my exam, I was happy.
  5 When my mother was born, her family moved to Glasgow. / Her family moved to Glasgow when my mother was born.
1 1 her
  2 it
  3 them/to him
  4 We, it
  5 him, him, them
2 1 My parents gave me their old car. / My parents gave their old car to me.
  2 Sarah saw John/him in the supermarket.
  3 Our teacher explained object pronouns to us. / Our teacher explained them to us.
  4 My brother won a prize. He won the prize / it in a spelling competition.
  5 We bought him a present. / We bought a present for him.

UNIT 12
1 1 b 4 a
  2 a 5 a
  3 b
2 1 was; 'm/am going
  2 go; 'm/am meeting
  3 is; opening; want
  4 are giving
  5 'm/am going; Do (you) want
1 1 am going to get
  2 is going to give
  3 are, going to do
  4 am going to answer
  5 isn't/'s not going to be
  6 am not going to complain
2 1 No change possible
  2 Peter loves photography. He's going shopping for a new camera tomorrow.
  3 No change possible
  4 My friend from Australia is visiting next week.
  5 I'm meeting my friends at the cinema tonight.

Macmillan Education
4 Crinan Street
London N1 9XW
A division of Macmillan Publishers Limited

Companies and representatives throughout the world

ISBN 978-0-230-45760-7

Designed by emc design limited
Illustrated by Peter Cornwell pp46 (top), 54, 62, 94, 95, 102, 130, 159
162; Sally Elford pp30, 45, 74, 75, 107, 110, 145; Jan _____ antner (Beehive
Illustration) p46 (bottom); Eva Thimgren (The Organisation)
Williams (Sylvie Poggio Artists) pp6, 24, 70, 143, 14_____
Cover design by emc design limited
Cover photography by **Getty Images**/Reza Easta _____ Getty Images/
Tim Robberts
Picture research by Susannah Jayes
Cover and unit opener picture research by emc design limited

Authors' acknowledgements
The authors would like to thank the schools, teachers and students whose
input has been invaluable in preparing this new edition. They would also
like to thank the editorial and design teams at Macmillan for doing such a
great job of organising the material and bringing it to life.

The publishers would like to thank the following educators and ___
who reviewed materials and provided us with invaluable in_
feedback for the development of the Open Mind series:

Petra Florianová, Gymnázium, Praha 6, Arabská 14; In_
Universidad Nacional de Río Cuarto; Alison Greenwoo_
Bologna, Centro Linguistico di Ateneo; Roumyana Ya_
American College of Sofia; Táňa Jančaříková, SOŠ D_____ ague; Mari
Carmen Lafuente, Escuela Oficial de Idiomas Hospitalet, Barcelona; Alice
Lockyer, Pompeu Fabra University; Javier Roque Sandro Majul, Windmill
School of English; Paul Neale, Susan Carol Owens and Beverley Anne
Sharp, Cambridge Academy of English; Audrey Renton, Dubai Men's
College, Higher Colleges of Technology, UAE; Martin Stanley, British
Council, Bilbao; Luiza Wójtowicz-Waga, Warsaw Study Centre; Escuela
Oficial de Idiomas de Getxo; Cámara de Comercio de Bilbao; Universidad
Autónoma de Bellaterra; Escuela Oficial de Idiomas EOI de Barcelona;
University of Barcelona; Escuela Oficial de Idiomas Sant Gervasi.

The author and publishers would like to thank the following for permission
to reproduce their photographs:
Alamy/Mike Abraham p23(tcl), Blue Jean Images p28(cr), David Cairns
p84(A), CandyBox Images p12, andrew chittock p22(A), Cultura Creative
pp22(c), 117(tl), Steve Davey Photography p60(bcr), Laurent Davoust
p99(cr), Chad Ehlers p55(cml), Gyula Gyukli p29(tcr), Jane Hobson p22(I), Ice
Tea Media p9(tl), i love images/fitness p82(bcl), i love images/men's lifestyle
pp92(cr), 109(tcr), Image Asset Management Ltd. p136(br), Image Source
p33(cr), Image Source Plus p69(tcl), Incamerastock p149(cr), Juice Images
p22(E), Juniors Bildarchiv GmbH p84(c), Andrey Kekyalyaynen p39, Jon
Parker Lee p149(bl), Larry Lilac p21(D), Lusoimages - Technology p101(tm),
Francisco Martinez p133(bl), Mitja Mladkovic p98, moodboard p33(bcl), Eric
Nathan p22(H), OJO Images Ltd p22(J), ONOKY - Photononstop pp11(4),
151, Frank Paul p117(cr), PhotoAlto sas p81(cr), PhotosIndia.com LLC
p81(cl), PHOVOIR p22(D), Photo Researchers p134, Prisma Bildagentur AG
p111(cmr), Simon Ritter p117(tcr), Andres Rodriguez pp26, 144(tl), Dmitriy
Shironosov p144(tcmr), Spaces Images p44, Kumar Sriskandan pp13,
22(F), StockbrokerXtra p76(br), Tetra Images p36(bcl), Val Thoermer p144(tr),
Marc Tielemans p35(A), Wavebreak Media ltd pp29(bcl), 123(cml), H. Mark
Weidman Photography p69(cml), Adrian Weinbrecht p16(3), Westend61
GmbH p96(4), whiteboxmedia limited p96(3), World Religions Photo Library
p59, Maksym Yemelyanov p76(bc), Justin Kase zsixz p22(G), ZUMA Press,
Inc. p58; **Apple Computers**/Courtesy of Apple Computers p29(bcr);
Bananastock pp36(cm), 64(cr), 106(bcrr), Punchstock p106(bcl), **Brand X**
p106(rice); **Comstock Images** p106(cheese); **Corbis** pp36(bcr), 106(bcml),
Peter Adams p120(cr), Theo Allofs p126, Bettmann p132, Assembly/Blend
Images p69(cr), JGI/Jamie Grill/Blend Images p52(tr), 76(cml), Jose Luis
Pelaez, Inc./Blend Images p76(tr), Edward Bock p28(cl), Alex Holland/
cultura p56, A. Geh/F1 Online p74(b), Randy Faris p76(cr), Tim Klein/
Galeries p120(br), Patrik Giardino p123(br), Tabor Gus p103, Hero Images

pp24(br), 104(cr), 113, Jon Hicks p124(tr), I Love Images p36(bm), Gurpal
Singh Datta/India Picture p31, Helen King p28(cm), Bob Krist p124(cl), Dann
Tardif/LWA p48(E), Raul Touzon/National Geographic Society p128, Ocean
pp11(cr), 81(tr), Odilon Dimier/PhotoAlto p36(br), 121, Photomorgana
p105(tl), Ed Quinn p135, Radius Images p49(br), Shannon Stapleton/
Reuters p117(br), Ken Seet p34, JENS SCHMIDT/STOCK4B/Stock4B
p48(br), Sandro Vannini p129(cl); **Getty Images** pp27(cl,cm), 35(cm),
106(crisps, bananas, oranges, watermelon, dried beans, broccoli, corn,
bread), 123(cl), 130, 131, AFP pp82(cl,cr), 136(bcm), Alex and Laila p52(b),
altrendo images p73, Helen Ashford p48(F), Eric Audras p142(tr), Henk
Badenhorst p69(bm), Bibikow p64(b), Bloomberg via Getty Images p14,
35(B), 139, Brand X p72, Visit Britain/Britain on View p142(br), Marco Brivio
p125(t), Sean De Burca p47, Simon Butterworth p32, Peter Cade p36(cr),
Nano Calvo p28(bcm), Reggie Casagrande pp71(br), 105(br), Cavan Images
p109(tr), Comstock Images p37, craftvision p92, John Cumming p69(cmr),
Datacraft Co Ltd p69(tcml), Peter Dazeley p22(B), Digital Vision pp23(tcr),
48(B), FilmMagic pp25, 27(cr), Photo by FOX via Getty Images p86(tr),
Elena Genova p15, Jen Grantham p48(A), Daniel Grill p11(1), Stephen
Hayward p112(cl), Bruno De Hogues p69(tcr), Jack Hollingsworth p16(1),
Andrew Holt p140, Utah-based Photographer Ryan Houston p70(br),
_____ Howard p63, _____ & Les Jacobs p144(tcml), Cultura/Robin James
_____ Ke_____ ___es p144(tcr), Taylor S. Kennedy p144(cr), Shuji
_____ _____iel Krieger Photography p111(cml), Michael Krinke
_____ ein p16(4), Justin Lambert p69(cl), Photography by
_____, Ulla Lohman _____ _____ _____ (tmr), Brian
_____ _____lately p8_____ _____ _____Meitzel
p_____, Peter Muller p44(c_____ _____ _____
p35(cml), Rick Neves p5_____ _____ _____
Photodisc p94(b), P_____ _____ _____(cr),
Photo by Dona_____ _____ _____(cr), sebastian-
julian p20, Jo_____ _____pson p9(bl), Blend Images/
Ariel Skelle_____ _____, Steve Skinner Photography
p123(_____ _____ _____aphy p118, John Sones Singing Bowl
Medi_____ _____ _____12(cr), Kniel Synnatzschke pp68(cr), 76(bl),
Su_____ _____andalay pp32(cr), 40(cm), Freudenthal Verhagen
_____40(tcl), Garry Wade p11(3), Adrian Weinbrecht p48(c),
_____(tr), Simon Wilkinson p43, WireImage p82(cm), Yukmin
_____ _____es/Rick Gomez/Blend RF p40(tcr), Inti St Clair/Blend
_____mages/Cultura pp36(bcm), 149(t), Monty Rakusen/
_____TB Photo p55(B), Radius Images p111(cl); **Image**
_____ _____ ocolate cake, butter, bcr), 122(tr); **Istockphoto** pp28(bcr),
_____lan Publishers Ltd/Paul Bricknell Photography p87(1, 2),
Studio8 pp8(cr), 16(2), 56(bl), 60(tl), 116(br), 122(br), David Tolley p40(cr);
The National Archives p179 (r); **PHOTOALTO** p106(peas); **Photodisc**/
Getty Images p106(steak); **Photoshot**/EFE p136(cr), Xinhua p55(D); **Rex
Features**/Evening News p133(tr), c.20thC.Fox/Everett/TM & copyright
20th Century Fox p38(cmr), Courtesy Everett Collection pp38(cml), 128(cr),
136(tcr), CSU Archives/Everett Collection p129(bl), ©Universal/Everett
p38(cl), Globe Photos p129(tcr), Dan Graves p84(B), Hatami Collection
p129(cm), Charles Knight p129(tcl), Herbie Knott p129(cr), Eddie Mulholland
p81(bcl), Tony Nutley p129(tcm), Geoffrey Robinson pp116, 127, Sipa Press
pp21(2), 55(c), SNAP p38(cr), Startraks Photo p21(3), Carlo Tischler p55(A),
Rex Images/Unimedia Images p21(1); **Superstock**/Westend61 p70(bl);
Thinkstock/Digital Vision p9(cr), George Doyle p140(cr), 144(tcl), Fuse
p141(bl), George Doyle & Ciaran Griffin p101(tr), Hemera pp17(cl), 21(B),
106(chicken), 117(tcl), Jack Hollingsworth p76(bcr), Ingram Publishing
pp104, 106(milk), Istockphoto pp33(cm), 35(c), 36(tl), 40(tcm), 48(D), 64(tr),
69(bcl), 71(bc), 76(cmr), 79, 80, 80(cm), 81(tl), 82(bcr), 83, 93(tl,cr,cm,bl),
96(2), 101(tl,tcl,tcm,cl,cm), 106(yoghurt), 120(tc), 125(c), JupiterImages
pp8, 33(cl), 86(cr), 93(bm), David Levit Photography p40(cl), Ryan McVay
p99(cm), Martin Poole pp76(bcm), 93(tm), Christopher Robbins p105(tr),
Stockbyte pp21(A), 100(tcr), Top Photo Group p120(tr), Zoonar p101(cr);
Up the Resolution p106(potatoes); **www.flyboarding.co.uk** p55(tr); **Eleni
Yiannoulidou** p68.

Printed and bound in Thailand

2019 2018 2017 2016
11 10 9 8 7 6 5

Open Mind
Elementary

is a ground-breaking six-level general English course for adults which targets their language needs and provides them with the professional, academic and personal skills they need for success in the 21st century. The key features of the series are:

- **Life Skills:** Higher-order skills such as critical thinking, organisational and learning skills that students need in order to be successful in their professional, academic and everyday lives.
- **Language sub-skills** with tips to support the development of the four language skills.
- **Step-by-step approach to grammar** with grammar sections that provide a clear focus on the meaning, form and function of the language.
- **Focus on functional language** to help learners with their fluency and improve their speaking skills.
- **Independent learning** features throughout the course such as *Notice!*, *Reflect* and *How are you doing?* boxes to encourage learners to analyse their own progress.
- A range of **video material** and worksheets to support the themes and key language from the Student's Book.

Student's Components
- **Student's Book Pack:** Print Student's Book; webcode access to Student's Resource Centre; DVD with video
- **Student's Book Premium Pack:** Print Student's Book; webcode access to Student's Resource Centre and Online Workbook
- **Print Workbook Pack:** Print Workbook (available with or without key); Audio CD
- **Online Workbook:** Webcode access to the Online Workbook

Teacher's Components
- **Teacher's Book Premium Pack:** Print Teacher's Book; Class Audio CD; DVD with video; webcode access to Teacher's Resource Centre, Online Workbook and Presentation Kit

Resource Centres
- **Student's Resource Centre:** Class Audio MP3s; Video; Downloadable self-study video worksheets; Downloadable wordlists; and more…!
- **Teacher's Resource Centre:** includes everything from the Student's Resource Centre, plus: Downloadable class video worksheets; Extra Life Skills lesson plans; Unit, Mid-course, End-of course and Placement tests

COMMON EUROPEAN FRAMEWORK

| AI | **A2** | BI | BI+ | B2 | CI |

Level indicator is an exit level.

MACMILLAN
www.macmillanenglish.com

System requirements for online components

Windows			Apple Macintosh OS				
	Windows 7 & 8				10.7	10.8	10.9
CPU Speed (equivalent)	Any 2 GHz dual core processor or above.		CPU Speed (equivalent)	Any 2 GHz dual core processor or above.			
Browser	IE 9, 10, 11 / Firefox / Chrome		Browser	Safari 6			

Internet connection required
RAM: 1GB (32-bit), 2GB (64-bit), Display: 1024 x 768 pixels, 32-bit colour, Audio sound card

DVD Player (for DVD-Videos or enhanced DVD ROMs)

While the online components may work for other browsers, we encourage using the browsers specified in the system requirements.

For customer support please contact help@macmillan.com

ISBN 978-0-230-45828-4

9 780230 458284

www.macmillanopenmind.com

WordBlaze

RUN AUSTRALIA

Name:

Date started:

Date completed:

RUN
AUSTRALIA

463.8 KM –
11 MARATHONS

© Liz McPhail

© iStock.com/Exkalibur

© iStock.com/Duchman

© iStock.com/keiichihiki

Christmas Island

Nearest mainland
point is 1500 km

Broome

6 are

8 eer

WESTERN AUSTRALIA

7 ie ei

Perth

© iStock.com/Byronsdad

© iStock.com/shannonstent